Guerrant

Heemstede,
Holland
April 25, 1962

HOW MUCH IS THAT IN DOLLARS?

HOW MUCH

Art Buchwald

IS THAT IN DOLLARS?

ILLUSTRATIONS BY *Laszlo Matulay*

CLEVELAND AND NEW YORK

THE WORLD PUBLISHING COMPANY

PUBLISHED BY The World Publishing Company
2231 WEST 110TH STREET, CLEVELAND 2, OHIO

PUBLISHED SIMULTANEOUSLY IN CANADA BY
NELSON, FOSTER & SCOTT LTD.

Library of Congress Catalog Card Number: 61-15305

THIRD PRINTING

3WP1261

Contents

2. LA VIE POLITIQUE

3. LES TOURISTES ENCORE

4. PARIS

CONTENTS

5. ET APRÈS, HONG KONG

CONTENTS

Introduction

I'VE never kept it a secret that I came to Paris in 1948 on the GI Bill of Rights. As someone who served in the troubles of 1941 to 1945 I was entitled to study anywhere I wanted to, and when friends at the University of Southern California assured me the streets of Paris were paved with mattresses, I decided to finish up my last year of schooling there.

Many other ex-GIs had the same idea and we all lived pretty interesting lives, which someday I'd like to write about if I can ever get my wife's permission.

But while we were going to school, and partaking of the wines of the country, Congress passed the monumental Marshall Plan, which was sort of a GI Bill for countries. The Marshall Plan was to have a great effect on American diplomacy, the American dollar, and in many cases the ex-GI who happened to be studying in Paris at the time.

For it turned out that Paris had been chosen as headquarters for this dollar dispensary and the Marshall Plan grew so fast that there was a shortage of American personnel. So all my ex-GI friends decided to sacrifice their schooling and seventy-five dollars a month, and become guards, couriers, and mail-room boys for Uncle Sam. They were, as we liked to put it, "Working for the Government."

But they didn't stay guards, couriers, or mail-room boys for long. The Marshall Plan grew so fast that one day a young American might be a night watchman and the next day he might be heading up the Coal and Steel Industry of Liechtenstein.

A mail-room clerk in a matter of weeks would find himself behind a desk in a private office overlooking the Place de la Concorde, advising union leaders how to keep Com-

munists out of their syndicates, and it was not inconceivable
for a courier who had a girl friend in the Personnel Department to wind up advising a European country how to
modernize its rolling stock.

I think I was one of the few Americans in Paris who tried
to get a job at the Marshall Plan and failed. Perhaps I was
shooting too high. I heard there was an opening for someone to run a mimeograph machine and so I immediately
bought a white shirt and a tie, and rushed down to apply
for the job. But a friend of mine who also heard of the job
applied as well. He had *actually* run a mimeograph machine
in high school, and since he could discuss it so much better,
he got the appointment.

True to form, my friend, starting with one mimeograph
machine, was soon supervising three, then a department of
mimeograph machines, and less than eight months later he
was running two four-color printing presses worth a couple
of hundred thousand dollars each.

When they wouldn't have me as a mimeograph operator
I went down to the *New York Herald Tribune*'s Paris Edition
and applied for a job as a restaurant and night club columnist. As luck would have it, I was hired, and while I'd rather
be operating a printing shop, I guess working for a newspaper has its advantages. This book is an attempt to spell
out many of them, and to convince myself I did the right
thing.

There were times when I really regretted my decision. One
was in 1949 when I was visiting a friend of mine who was
in charge of new factories or some such thing for the Marshall Plan. This friend was a boy who only six months before
ate bread and cheese for lunch and dinner when he ran out
of GI Bill money. We used to go down to Les Halles together
at two or three in the morning and swipe vegetables and
fruit to keep us going until the end of the month.

Well, after this kind of life I suddenly found my friend
sitting behind this big metal desk, smoking a cigar and pushing buttons which brought pretty young French secretaries

to his feet while he dictated memos in triplicate to Washington, Tokyo, and Nome, Alaska.

Finally, a French manufacturer was ushered into his presence and as I stared in amazement the Frenchman explained that he wanted to build a factory outside of Lyon and all he needed to get the project going was two hundred million francs.

My friend stared at him coldly and said, "How much is that in dollars?"

It was the first time my friend ever saw me cry.

1. La Famille Buchwald

Hagerty Was Here

AMONG the more distinguished members of the press who were in Paris when President John F. Kennedy arrived last spring was Mr. James Hagerty, the former press secretary of the former President of the United States.

Mr. Hagerty came in connection with his new job as vice-president in charge of public affairs of the American Broadcasting Company.

Now, a lot of my colleagues were rubbing their hands with glee at the thought of my meeting Mr. Hagerty again, because the last time we saw each other was in November 1958, in Paris, at which time we had words, many of them printed in the world's newspapers.

If my colleagues expected me to resume these words when Mr. Hagerty arrived, they were disappointed. I have nothing but warm feelings for Mr. Hagerty, and he has done more for me than any living Presidential press secretary I know.

Look at it from my standpoint. Before Mr. Hagerty decided to single me out from the vast multitude of the press corps, and said I wrote "unadulterated rot," I was a poor, struggling syndicated columnist who didn't know where his next newspaper was coming from. My wife owned a cloth coat and my children had to go to public schools.

Although we had a nurse and cook, we could only afford a part-time cleaning woman. Things were very rough for us, and I was thinking of chucking the whole thing and getting a high-paying job with the CIA.

Then Mr. Hagerty, as he himself has since admitted, lost his temper, and by the strangest quirk of luck he lost it on me.

There I was, sitting in the briefing hall of the Crillon

Hotel, jammed in with the cream of the White House press corps, surrounded by men who not only had so much more experience and stature, but some who had triple my syndication—and suddenly Mr. Hagerty said the magic words "unadulterated rot."

At first I couldn't believe he was talking about me, not because I don't write unadulterated rot, but because I was a stranger to Mr. Hagerty, and the rest of the reporters were his friends.

As George Dixon, the syndicated Washington columnist, wrote at the time, with jealousy and bitterness: "I've been writing unadulterated rot for years and Hagerty's never picked on me."

Well, you don't look a gift horse in the mouth and, I said to myself, if the press secretary of the President of the United States wants to help me with my career why should I interfere with his plans? I kept quiet and thanks to Mr. Hagerty I picked up fourteen newspapers who had no interest in the column before, my wife now has a new mink coat, the children go to a private school, and we now have a *full-time* cleaning woman. If it hadn't been for Mr. Hagerty none of this would have happened, so, I ask you, why should I be mad at him?

The guy who could do me some good by getting mad at me is Pierre Salinger, President Kennedy's press secretary. Just one word about unadulterated rot from him and I'd be able to afford to send the children to Harvard.

But it's too much to hope for. Anyway, there is no reason for Salinger to help me, because he probably figures, like everybody else, that Hagerty's done enough for me already.

So if anyone thought there was going to be any fireworks when Mr. Hagerty came over they were sorely disappointed. As a matter of fact what I really would have liked to have done was take him to the Lido with my wife—fur coat and all.

How I Became the Boss in My Family

As I AM an American father of an American wife with three American children, people are constantly amazed to discover that I am the boss in my family. This I know is a complete switch from the trend and many people have tried to ascribe it to the fact that I live in Paris and don't have the pressure on me that most American males do in the United States.

But I refuse to believe this is true. I know that if I lived in the United States I would still be the boss of the family, and it's not just because I beat my wife either.

Being the boss in the family is just a state of mind.

One of my favorite stories on the subject concerns a reporter who went out to interview a man on his golden anniversary. The reporter asked the man, "To what do you credit your long years of happy marriage?"

The man replied, "We have been happily wed for all these years because my wife has always made the small decisions and I have always made the big ones."

"For example?" the reporter wanted to know.

"Well, my wife decides what clothes I should wear, what food I should eat, where I should work, when I should take my vacation, who my friends should be, when I should go to sleep, and when I should wake up in the morning."

The reporter was astonished. "Those are the small decisions? Then what are the decisions *you* make?"

The man said "I decide who the President of the United States is going to be, questions on the Congo, the Middle East and Quemoy and Matsu, and all matters concerning disarmament."

I first became boss of the family about two years ago and it was quite by accident. Up until then like all American husbands and fathers I had been the stereotyped head of the house, the butt of all the jokes, the good-natured long-suffering male who, because I supplied the bacon, was constantly being put in the frying pan.

And like all American males I didn't seem to mind the role, probably because I didn't know any better.

But then a strange thing happened. I came home one day from the office to discover what is known in France as a Crise de Ménage (A crisis in the house). Everyone from my dear wife to my three little children to the nurse and the cook was up in arms.

It seems the concierge (which in France is a combination of building superintendent, Gestapo agent, and mother-in-law) had insulted the cook and had called her a "name." The cook said she would not work in an apartment house with such a blankety blank and was leaving. My wife was upset and said, "This time the concierge has gone too far and I'm not going to stand for it."

The children all agreed, though they had no idea what anyone was talking about. The nurse said she too was fed up with the concierge and everyone turned to me to see what I was going to do about it, though it was obvious by their expressions they didn't expect much.

My first instinct was to defend the concierge on the grounds that she was old and deaf, and since she was just mean by nature it seemed useless to take offense.

But before I opened my trap I realized this would be useless and all I would receive for my peacemaking efforts was the usual contempt and scorn from my loved ones.

So, much to their surprise, I said, "This is the last straw. No one is going to insult *my* cook and get away with it. I'm going to have it out with her once and for all."

I stormed out of the apartment breathing fire and brimstone and descended to the ground floor where the concierge lived. I found her stirring her witches' broth with a broomstick. She snarled politely, "Oui, Monsieur."

I stared at her and then I put my hand in my pocket

and took out twenty francs (four dollars) and I said as I held the francs out, "Why did you insult the cook?"

She took the francs and said, "I didn't mean to insult the cook."

"That's what I told her," I said. "You won't insult her again, will you?"

She put the money into a drawer hastily and replied, "Of course not, Monsieur. Be assured of it."

I stalked upstairs, where the entire family was waiting anxiously for the results.

"Well, I fixed that one," I said triumphantly. "She'll never insult the cook again."

"What did you say to her?" my wife asked in what seemed for the first time to be a tone of admiration.

"I can't tell you in front of the children," I replied. "But I gave her *more* than a piece of my mind."

The entire family seemed to be thrilled with the results and I could feel a wave of respect sweep through the apartment such as I had never felt before.

A week later I had another chance to show who was boss. The children go to school in Paris and the school bus had just been rerouted so our children had to walk five blocks every morning to catch it, whereas in the past they had to only walk a block.

This irritated my wife and the nurse and it was suggested I go to school and speak to the principal about it.

I said I would first speak to the bus driver and if I got no satisfaction from him I would take it up with the principal.

The next morning I walked the five blocks to the bus stop and waited with the three children. When the bus came I asked if I could speak to the driver a minute. As he stepped down I had palmed fifty francs (ten dollars) in my hand, and when we shook hands he accepted the money with the calmness and lack of expression of a headwaiter in a leading French restaurant.

I explained five blocks seemed a long walk for the children and he couldn't have agreed more. He thought he could probably reroute the bus so it could stop in front of our house so the children wouldn't even have to walk the block they did in the past.

When I got home that night an entire cheering squad was waiting for me.

"How did you do it?" asked my beaming wife.

"No bus driver is going to push our children around," I said. "I just told him off."

Things at home started to pick up for me. I was even called in on decisions about the house and I was asked about my opinion on political matters.

A few weeks later I was called in again on an important matter. I arrived home from the office and my wife said:

"Joel is impossible. He kicked the nurse, he's hitting his sisters all the time, he won't do his homework, and he won't go to bed. I can't do a thing with him. He needs some discipline."

"You're damn right he does," I said, "and I'm going to see he gets it."

I grabbed him by the arm and took him into his room and slammed the door.

"Now," I said angrily, "how much is it worth to you to be a good boy and stop kicking the nurse, hitting your sisters, and going to bed late?"

"Huh?" he said.

"How much do you want? No questions asked. What's the going rate for being a good boy?"

"I don't know." he said honestly.

"Would twenty-five francs be enough?"

"Every week?"

"Well that seems a lot for a seven-year-old boy."

"Every week," he said, "or it's no deal."

"Okay, okay, but not so loud. One thing though. You have to apologize to the nurse."

"That's extra," he said.

"You're blackmailing me," I cried.

"I won't apologize unless you give me ten francs more."

"All right," I said. "But don't tell anyone you're getting this money. It's a secret, right?"

"Yes," he said.

"Now start screaming as though I've beaten you."

Joel started to scream and I walked out of his room rolling down my sleeves. His mother and sisters and the nurse looked terrified.

"You didn't hurt him?" my wife wanted to know anxiously.

I snickered and refused to reply.

A few nights later Joel bragged to his sisters about his payoff and I had to start paying them to keep quiet.

Pretty soon the nurse got wind of the windfall the children were getting and demanded a raise which I could hardly refuse under the circumstances.

Now everyone seemed to respect me except my wife, who still had doubts that I was the captain of the ship. But I changed that overnight.

One evening I came home from a gin rummy game flushed with victory and declared that from now on I would give her 10 per cent of my winnings. In the past my wife has always resented my gin rummy playing, but now that she had a stake in it she took an added interest.

As far as she is concerned I haven't lost a game since that evening though I have to admit what with my losses and 10 per cent of my fictional "winnings" going out every week it's been costing me hundreds of dollars. I've been doing so badly in fact that I would probably quit the game but since I've been "winning" so much I can't think of any reason to tell my wife why I want to stop playing.

So, for the past two years I've been giving the concierge twenty francs a month not to insult the cook, the bus driver fifty francs a month so he'll stop in front of the apartment, my son twenty-five francs a week so he won't hit his sisters, his sisters ten francs a week each so they won't tell his mother that I'm paying him, the nurse a raise of twenty dollars a month, and my wife 10 per cent of gin winnings I never had.

It's been a very expensive period for me but it's been

worth it. What other American father can truly say he is boss of the family with no questions asked?

Anyone for Hamburger?

I ALMOST had dinner with the Vice-President of the United States, Lyndon Johnson, and it was almost one of the greatest evenings I ever spent in Paris.

This is what happened. The Vice-President and his wife had arrived to spend one day and night in Paris and asked a very good friend of theirs, who also happens to be a very good friend of mine, if he would select a restaurant to give the dinner. My friend called me up and said: "How would you like to have dinner with the Vice-President of the United States and his wife?"

I said it would be nice.

"Well, I haven't cleared it with them yet, but I'm sure it will be all right. What restaurant should we dine at?"

"Why don't you reserve at Novy's? It's got White Russian music and a nice atmosphere."

"Good idea," he said.

"Where shall we meet?" I asked excitedly.

"At the ambassador's."

"What ambassador?" I asked.

"Haven't you been invited to the cocktail party the Gavins are giving for the Vice-President?"

"No," I said.

"Well, I'll call the embassy and tell them you're going to have dinner with the Vice-President and I'm sure they'll invite you."

"Gee, that's swell," I said.

I couldn't wait to telephone my wife and tell her. But she wasn't home and I told our cook, Danielle, to tell my wife as soon as she came in that we were having dinner with the Vice-President of the United States.

A few minutes later the American Embassy called and said they would be very happy to have me come to a cocktail party the ambassador was giving for the Vice-President.

I said I'd be very happy to go.

Then I went out to lunch and told everyone I met I couldn't have dinner with them because I was dining with the Lyndon Johnsons.

In the meantime my wife had come home and when Danielle told my wife about our dinner plans, she dashed out of the house and rushed off to Alexandre's, the famous Paris coiffeur, to get her hair done.

Alexandre's is a very fashionable place and you can't get in without an appointment. But when my wife explained she was going to have dinner with the Vice-President of the United States, they threw a duchess out the window and gave my wife her chair.

Meanwhile, back at the office, I was reading up on protocol and the great Vice-Presidents of our country when the phone rang, and it was my friend, who was so embarrassed he could hardly talk. It seems the Johnsons had insisted on a small dinner party made up of just their friends, and he said he couldn't invite me.

"That's okay," I said, trying to keep my tears away from the mouthpiece. "Let's do it some other time."

"I'm terribly sorry," he said. "I should have asked them before I asked you."

"Really, it's nothing," I blubbered. "I'll be happy to stay in and read a good book."

"But aren't you coming to the cocktail party?" he asked.

"We can't," I said. "The reason we were invited to the cocktail party was because we were going to dinner with the Vice-President. We'd feel like impostors if we showed up for drinks and weren't going on."

"I guess you're right," he said and hung up.

Five minutes later my wife called up, deliriously happy. "Hi," she said, "this is quite a day. One minute we're going to eat hamburgers at home for dinner, and the next we're going out with the Vice-President of the United States."

"WAIT A MINUTE, SOCIAL CLIMBER!" I shouted. Then I explained quietly what had happened.

"But what will I tell them the next time I go to Alexandre's?" she cried.

"You can fake it. They'll never know."

"What about Danielle? She's told everyone in the neighborhood. What can I tell her?"

"Tell her . . . tell her . . . not to throw the hamburgers away."

Why We're Envied

ONE of the things Americans in the United States envy Americans who live in Paris for is the fact that those of us who live abroad are not saturated with television.

"We can't get our kids away from the television set," my friends complain. "At least your kids live a normal life."

If by living a normal life my friends mean that instead of watching television our kids are kept busy breaking all the furniture in the home, then I guess they have a point.

But I'd rather have my kids ruined by television then give them a chance to ruin the apartment.

Two years ago I bought a French television set and I've been watching it intermittently ever since. I say intermittently because I'm never quite sure when there is going to be a program on the air. On some days there is television from 11:30 A.M. until 1:30 P.M. Then it goes off again until 6:30 or 7:30 P.M., except on Thursdays, Saturdays, and Sundays when there is a football game, unless the game is not allowed to be televised because it is being played in Paris and the promoters are afraid it will cut the gate.

There have been times when I've stared at a large clock for thirty minutes straight, and for a while there was a program consisting of nothing but waves washing up on the sands, with music in the background. I watched this program every week hoping that one day I'd see a fish, but it never happened.

There is only one television channel in Paris and that is owned lock, stock, and antenna by the French government.

As far as programs for children are concerned the French don't seem to be too interested.

Last Sunday, after a very late Saturday night, I sent my three housewreckers in to look at the television set.

It was 2:30 and they returned from the dining room where we keep the set.

"There's nothing on," they complained.

"There must be something on," I said, "I hear sound."

I went to look and discovered that the National Television Orchestra was playing Claude Debussy's "La Mer," without waves, that is.

The kids proceeded to destroy a tea table that had suddenly become an Indian fort.

At three o'clock I sent them back into the dining room.

They returned at 3:02. "There's nothing on."

I went to see. It was a cross-country race at Nantes. Even I tired of it after the second mile.

The Indians surrounded the fort and broke two lamps trying to shoot down their sister.

At 5:02 I heard the woman announcer tell everyone to stand by for a film.

I looked up the film in the newspaper program, and there in black letters it said, "Humphrey Bogart in *Echec à la Gestapo*. FOR ADULTS ONLY."

So much for television on a quiet Sunday afternoon.

But I don't want to give the impression everything on French television is for adults. At ten one night there was an international circus from Brussels. I became so excited I woke the kids up to let them watch it, but instead of thanking me, they cried.

Even the films shown "For Adults Only" aren't necessarily for *all* adults. Last Sunday at 8:30 P.M. the French showed *Bitter Rice*, but in the television program magazine, viewers were informed that Catholic censors didn't recommend it.

The most fun on French TV is provided by the sports events, particularly the international football and soccer matches, in which France plays another country. The French announcers are rather chauvinistic about the home team and make such remarks as, "That's the worst referee I've ever seen. Look what he's doing to the poor French team." Or, when there is a foul against the French, the announcer will shout, "Where's the referee? Where's the referee?"

A score for France is always "magnifique" and for the foreign team "tant pis" ("tough luck").

Sometimes the announcer gets so excited that no one has any idea what has happened. All he keeps screaming is "Zut alors, zut alors, quel dommage, quel dommage, mais non, mais non, mais non." This means, as anyone who watches French television knows, that the French have just failed to score.

But except for sports, we're willing to trade five plays by the Comédie-Française for one half-hour of *Wagon Train*. Just think of the money we'd save on furniture.

Un-American Baseball in Paris

IT SEEMS that every other letter I get these days from friends who happen to be fathers of young boys has to do with their sons' achievements in Little League baseball.

"David hit a home run with bases loaded," one father wrote proudly.

"Billy pitched a one-hit game and won the Roslyn Player of the Year Award," another father informed me modestly.

Another letter said: "The coach who hates my guts, won't let Jimmy play, and I'm going to officially protest at the next Little League meeting."

It appears from the mail that fathers take Little League baseball very seriously, and heaven help the kid who doesn't live up to his father's expectations.

There are Little Leagues in Europe, but they are at Army and Air Force bases and don't differ at all from the leagues in the United States.

But for those American fathers who live in and around Paris, Little League doesn't exist. As a matter of fact, baseball hardly exists at all. But the other day at a cocktail party, a group of fathers decided to have a picnic and baseball game to introduce their sons to the great national sport.

We got together eight couples and nobody knows how many children. One of the fathers had a baseball bat, and another, through military connections, managed to get a softball at the PX.

We drove out in cavalcade to the Bois de Boulogne, trying to find an area that might suffice for a diamond. We found one near the pigeon-shooting range. There were a few French picnickers in the area, but there was plenty of room for everybody.

While the women laid out the picnic equipment, the fathers laid out the bases. No one was quite sure how much distance there was supposed to be between the bases, and a few fathers, who hadn't been back to the United States in several years, weren't even quite sure how many bases were needed.

One of the fathers insisted that when he played there were only *three* bases, including home plate. But another father, who had just returned from home leave, assured us we needed four bases, and we decided to take his word for it.

The first half-hour was spent in explaining to our sons the object of the game. The older ones said they'd rather play soccer, and the younger ones insisted they wanted to eat.

Since there was a manpower shortage, the wives were recruited as players. We chose up sides and in order to give all the children a chance to play, we wound up with twelve players on one team and thirteen on the other.

It was agreed that we wouldn't count runs or outs of any players under eight years of age.

The first thing we discovered was that the softball was too

hard for everybody. So, instead, I took a rubber ball away from my five-year-old daughter, Jennifer, who screamed to high heaven. She was making such a racket that my wife, who was playing shortstop, was thrown out of the game and had to sit with her. But it was just as well. With my wife out, it evened up the sides.

At first our sons were interested in what was happening. But when they discovered that all they were supposed to do was stand around in the outfield, they became bored and started wrestling with each other. Several disappeared into the woods to climb trees.

The only time they would come out of the woods was when it was their turn to bat.

The French picnickers became very interested in the game and asked many questions. I'm not certain if they understood everything.

At one point in the game there were three children on first base, a French poodle literally trying to steal second base, and the center fielder talking a policeman out of giving him a ticket for parking on the grass.

The final score was 29 to 23, but no one was quite sure which side won.

Although it wasn't Little League baseball, I'm certain we created an interest in our sons in the game.

Just last night my boy said to me: "When are we going out again to the Bois and play that game, you know, the one with the stick and Jennifer's rubber ball?"

I can't wait to write to my friends back home.

The Good and the Bad

I took my son to the movies the other day. The picture was called *The Battle of the Coral Sea,* and in comparison with other war pictures it was pretty bad. It had something to do with a crew of American submariners who are captured by the Japanese and are put in a prison camp. The man in charge of the prison camp is a very civilized man, by prison camp standards, and he resists torturing his charges even though he knows they know naval secrets that could change the course of the war. But the people under the commander are typical brutal prison guards.

There is no sense going on with the plot except to say it was no *Bridge on the River Kwai*.

When we got out of the theater we went to a sidewalk café to have a drink. My son was pretty quiet after the film and it had left a deep impression on him.

At the table he said to me: "The Japanese were very bad people to do those things to the Americans, weren't they?"

"Yes," I said, "but they're not bad people now."

"Why?" he wanted to know.

"Because they don't do things like that any more."

He thought about this a minute and then said: "Why did they do all those bad things then?"

"Probably they didn't know they were doing bad things. They probably thought they were doing good things."

"Why didn't someone tell them?" he wanted to know.

"We tried," I said, "but they wouldn't listen."

"Remember that war picture we saw some weeks ago? The one about the Germans and how they beat the poor people and the children in the prison camp?"

"Yes," I said.

"The Germans are bad people, aren't they?"

"No," I said. "They *were* bad people, but now they're good people."

"Are they different people?" he wanted to know.

"No, they're the same people. At least many are the same people. You see, once you fight a war you can't stay mad at the people after the war is over. You have to forget what the bad people did during the war, because if you don't there could be another war."

"But in the movies they're still bad people," he said.

"Yes. That's to remind us they were bad people, but we're supposed to forget it."

He looked at me blankly.

"Did you kill any Russians during the war?" he wanted to know a few minutes later.

"No. Because during the war they were good people and they fought the Germans just like the British and the Americans did."

"But, if they were good people during the war and killed the bad people, why are they bad people now?"

"They're not bad now. Most of the Russians are good people. But we don't agree with what their leaders say and want to do. And they don't agree with us. That's why we're having trouble in Germany."

"With the bad Germans?"

"No, with the good Germans. The bad Germans want to kick the good Germans out of Berlin."

"Then there are still bad Germans?"

"Yes. But there are also good Germans. You see, after the war the country was divided and the Russians occupied half of it and we occupied the other half."

"Why didn't the Russians kill the bad Germans if they were bad?"

"Well, the Russians don't think their Germans are bad. They think their Germans are good. They think our Germans are bad. We think their Germans, at least their German leaders, are bad, and our Germans are good. You understand?"

He said: "No."

"Well, it doesn't make any difference if you understand it or not," I said angrily. "Everyone else does. I never saw a kid who asked so many silly questions."

The Family Gold Deficit

PRESIDENT KENNEDY'S dramatic edict about our gold reserves will eventually affect every American at home and abroad. The loss of dollars and gold from the United States comes as no surprise to me, as I have been telling my wife for years that she has been spending far too many dollars in Paris and one of these days the President was going to hear about it.

On my recent trip to the United States I took my wife with me and she spent so much money in New York department stores that for a few minutes there I thought she was going to restore the balance of trade single-handed.

But either President Kennedy made his decision before my wife started shopping or our gold reserves are lower than everyone thinks, because our recent spending spree doesn't seem to have had any effect on the President's decision to bring the United States back in economic shape.

As a good American, who makes his home in France, I felt that some effort should be made to stop the flow of gold out of the United States, and the best place to start was right in our home.

I called a meeting of the family, including my wife, the three children, aged seven, six, and five, the French cook, and the Irish nurse. It was hoped that the Secretary of the Treasury would stop by the house to explain the deficit situation to the family in terms they would understand, but unfortunately he had to fly straight on to West Germany to explain it to Chancellor Adenauer.

So I had to take over.

"Your mother," I said, "has caused a gold deficit in the United States."

My wife tried to protest but we ruled her out of order.

"Before I married her, the United States had $30,000,000,-000 in gold reserves. Now, after eight years of marriage, the United States has only $18,000,000,000. It is obvious that this family is buying far more than we're selling, and something has to be done about it."

My wife protested. "I have only spent money that would prevent the family from *looking* like Communists. Our investment abroad has paid dividends in many ways. Our prestige is at an all-time high. We have three times as many friends as we had eight years ago, and a day doesn't go by when someone doesn't call and ask us when we're going to give another party."

The children looked to me for a reply.

I said: "I don't object to spending money on necessities such as cocktail parties, new lamps for the living room, paintings by young 'undiscovered' French artists, and ballet lessons for the girls. We all know this is money well spent.

"But I do object to throwing dollars down the drain for shoes, the school bus, hot water, heat, and food. We have nothing to show for this money, and the people we give it to are probably laughing behind our backs."

My seven-year-old son said, "Daddy's right. I don't think I should go to school. That's where most of the money is going."

"Now you've started something," my wife said.

I called the meeting back to order. "I think we'll still let the children go to school. The savings will have to be made in the house. First, we must start a 'Buy American' program and purchase American goods wherever we can."

I addressed the cook: "For example, Danielle, why can't we have Campbell's tomato soup for dinner instead of French soup?"

Danielle got up and left the room.

"Where's she going?" I asked my wife.

"To pack her bags."

"Well," I said, "that's a large dollar-saving right there."

My wife started to leave the room.

"Where are you going?" I demanded.

"To pack my bags."

The children followed her out as did the nurse.

I was left alone trying to solve Kennedy's monetary problems.

It looked as if I would get no co-operation at home, so I dropped my gold wedding band into an envelope and mailed it to the White House. At least the President will know I cared.

New Cooking Frontiers

I CAME home from the office the other day at six o'clock in the evening to find my wife pacing nervously up and down.

"What's wrong?" I asked.

"Danielle went out to the butcher shop at five o'clock and she's not back yet."

Danielle, our cook, has been with us for four years, and she makes a mean soufflé, an unbelievable Poulet de Bresse, and a wild, wild canard with peaches which is out of this world. She is not temperamental, she likes children, and she'll work late if we ask her to.

I was surprised at my wife's concern.

"She's only been gone an hour. What are you so nervous about?"

"Don't you read the newspapers?" my wife asked angrily.

"Sure I read the newspapers," I said.

"Well, then, you know why I am worried."

"You mean you think that THEY might have . . ."

"I don't know what to think," she said.

"But we're Americans. THEY wouldn't steal a cook from Americans. The French Ambassador to London is one thing . . ."

"I'm not making any accusations. All I know is Danielle saw THEM on French television the other night and she said THEY looked like very, very nice people."

"But," I protested, "that doesn't mean anything. All our French friends think THEY'RE nice people."

"This is not our friends," my wife said. "This is our cook."

"It is true she's been acting funny lately," I said. "I mean nothing you could put your finger on. I remember the other night she asked if she could find American cake mix in France, but I didn't think anything of it at the time."

"Two days ago," my wife said, "I bumped into her only two blocks from the American Embassy. She said she was going to the Galeries Lafayette, but she looked awfully nervous."

"I saw her cutting out a picture of Caroline from *Paris-Match*," I said.

My wife started to sob.

"But wait a minute," I said, trying to comfort her. "Let's not jump to any conclusions. First of all, how could THEY have even found out about Danielle?"

"How did THEY find out about the French Ambassador's chef?" she said, twisting her handkerchief.

She had a point.

"Has she gotten any mail from Washington lately?" I asked.

"No, but THEY could have written to her in care of a friend."

"What about long-distance telephone calls?"

"I don't believe so. But we've been out so much THEY could have called when we weren't here," my wife said.

"Perhaps if we gave her a raise?"

"How could we compete against HIS father's millions?" she replied.

"Well, I guess we better prepare for the worst."

Just then Danielle returned and we both jumped up and rushed to her.

"I've been thinking it over and I think I'll do it," she said.

"Do what?" my wife asked.

"I'll use the leftover beef and make a ragout. The children love it."

Danielle stared in amazement as both of us laughed hysterically.

My Wife the Duchess

MY WIFE was scrubbing the floor the other day and it suddenly occurred to me that she hadn't bought any clothes in
a long time. The nice thing about my wife is that she never
complains about clothes, like some women I know.

If she doesn't have any clothes to wear she always says:
"All right, I'll go to Maxim's in my slip."

But I decided to take pity on her, and as soon as she
mopped up I said: "How would you like to see the Christian
Dior collection?"

"What for?" she said as she rinsed out the pail.

"Maybe there is something in the new collection that
you'd like to buy. The fashion critics say it's very beautiful."

"You mean to say you'd buy me some clothes at Christian
Dior?" she said.

"Of course," I replied. "I like my wife to be well dressed
just as much as the Duke of Windsor likes his wife to be
well dressed. What's good enough for the duchess is good
enough for you. Let's go now. There's a showing at ten
o'clock this morning."

She was so excited she almost forgot to put the pail away.

She put her coat on in record time and we were just
leaving when I said: "Don't you think you'd better take your
apron off? I'd understand, but you know what snobs those
fashion people are."

She took off her apron and away we went. "You're not
fooling me now about letting me buy a Christian Dior dress,
are you?"

"Of course, I'm not fooling," I assured her. "Anything your
little heart desires. Just pretend you're the duchess and I'm
the duke."

The salons of Christian Dior were jammed, but we were

given two of the best seats in the house. Obviously we had the look of big spenders written all over our faces.

The show started and my wife, her eyes sparkling, was thrilled. First came the spring suits and everyone "ahhhed" and "ohhhed."

A lovely number called Bois de Boulogne (that was the name of the dress, not the model) came out, and my wife tugged my arm. "That one, I like that one."

"Wonderful," I said. "When would you wear it? To take the children to the dentist or meet them when they come home on the school bus?"

My wife didn't say anything.

Fifteen minutes later she saw an orange suede suit. "Oh," she said, "I'd give anything to have that suede suit. It would be wonderful for the afternoon."

"Then you shall have it. I don't think that the fact that Joel gets car-sick should stand in the way of your owning the suit. I understand they can clean suede without any trouble these days."

"Never mind," my wife said.

"There's a nice cocktail dress," I said a few moments later. "And you could use one for Connie's birthday party. After all, your other one was ruined at Jennifer's with all that ice cream and cake that was spilled on it."

My wife started to lose interest.

"Would you like a new spring coat," I suggested, "to wear when you have to visit the principal about the kids' grades? That blue one's nice, but it's a little too formal to wash the car in. I'd suggest an evening gown, but since sitters are so hard to get, it hardly seems worth the money. But don't let me influence you. Anything *you* like *you* get."

"Let's forget it," my wife said. "I don't really want any new clothes. I'm very happy with what I've got. There's only one thing I'd like you to buy for me."

"What's that?" I wanted to know.

"A new pail," she said bitterly.

"Sure, what kind?"

"The same kind the Duchess of Windsor has."

The Mothers-in-Law

MY MOTHER-IN-LAW is back in Paris making an on-the-spot investigation for the United Nations of conditions at my house, where several factions have been fighting for supremacy since my three children came back from their Swiss vacation.

Inadvertently my mother-in-law made me lose a lifelong friend, Alain Bernheim, and I have only myself to blame.

This is what happened.

Anatole Litvak, the director, was about to make a film in Paris called *Goodbye Again* with Ingrid Bergman, Yves Montand, and Tony Perkins, and to launch his film he held a press cocktail party at the Hotel George V.

My mother-in-law is a big fan of Miss Bergman's and so I took her to the party. Miss Bergman was very gracious and my mother-in-law was thrilled. She also met Sam Taylor, who wrote the script for *Goodbye Again* and he invited us both to dinner at the Plaza Athénée after the press party. As luck would have it, his date was Miss Bergman.

Well, you can imagine how thrilled my mother-in-law was—not only to meet Miss Bergman, but to have dinner with her.

To make matters even better, James Stewart, who was staying at the Plaza, stopped by to say hello to Miss Bergman and so my mother-in-law met him too. Celebrity-wise speaking, it was a memorable evening in my mother-in-law's life and I went to bed happy in the knowledge that Warren, Pennsylvania, would soon have a firsthand report on Ingrid Bergman, James Stewart, Tony Perkins, and Yves Montand.

But unfortunately the next day my mother-in-law had a luncheon date with Mr. Bernheim's mother-in-law, Mrs. Lillian Kessler, of Los Angeles. Somehow, I'll never know how, my mother-in-law mentioned to Mr. Bernheim's mother-in-law where she had been on the previous evening and also whom she had met.

As I understand it, my mother-in-law laid it on pretty thick and no matter how Mrs. Kessler kept trying to change the subject, my mother-in-law kept coming back to "Ingrid," "Jimmy," "Tony," and "Yves."

That evening Mrs. Kessler confronted her son-in-law, who used to be my best friend, at the dinner table, and said: "Marie McGarry's son-in-law took *her* to dinner with Ingrid Bergman."

Mr. Bernheim flushed.

"He also introduced her to James Stewart, Tony Perkins, Yves Montand, and some Taylor, probably Elizabeth. It's funny that you don't introduce me to anybody except some of your wild French friends."

Mr. Bernheim protested: "I introduced you to Paulette Goddard in Ascona."

Mrs. Kessler said: "She's not Ingrid Bergman."

Mr. Bernheim said: "I knew Bergman before Mrs. McGarry's son-in-law knew her."

Mrs. Kessler said: "The difference is he introduced her to Mrs. McGarry, but you would never think of introducing me to her."

"It's not true," Mr. Bernheim protested. "The next time I see Miss Bergman I'll introduce her."

"Yes," said Mrs. Kessler. "But will she go to dinner with me, like she did with Mrs. McGarry?"

"I can't promise that," Mr. Bernheim said.

"I thought so," Mrs. Kessler said. "There are some sons-in-law that care more about their mothers-in-law than other sons-in-law."

Mr. Bernheim was starting to feel pretty bad, but Mrs. Kessler wouldn't let up on him.

"She said icily, "Do you know Jimmy?""

"Jimmy who?" Mrs. Bernheim asked.

"I thought so," said Mrs. Kessler. "You start and stop with Paulette Goddard."

At this point Mr. Bernheim couldn't take it any more and he went to the phone. On the basis of what my mother-in-law had told me, I was expecting his call.

"What the hell are you doing to me?" he screamed.

"I'm sorry," I said. "How did I know my mother-in-law would talk?"

"After all I've done for you," he sobbed, "this is how you repay me."

"Look," I suggested, "Why don't you take her to dinner with Paulette Goddard?"

Mr. Bernheim hung up on me. I never knew him to be such a sore loser.

Behind Every Man

BEHIND every man there's a woman, and it's true of me just as it is of the President of the United States. My wife has always been of valuable help to me in everything I've tried to accomplish, and I don't mind saying it publicly.

Take, for example, last night, when an insurance man came over to the house to assess our possessions. I don't know what I would have done without her.

The insurance man brought with him an expert in home furnishings whose word, as far as Lloyd's of London is concerned, is as good as gold, and we started taking inventory.

I gave the insurance man a list of what I estimated the value of our possessions to be, and all I wanted was confirmation from him. Naturally one exaggerates a little in these matters, but it's good for Lloyd's business and they usually take these exaggerations into consideration.

The first thing the expert looked at was a pair of lamps.

"I see you have those lamps valued at one hundred dollars," he said.

"But, darling," my wife said, "I only paid thirty dollars

for them at the Flea Market. You remember I came home and you were so pleased with the bargain."

The expert crossed out the $100 and put $30 in its place.

I smiled sickly at my wife and said: "I must have forgotten."

"That table over there I brought from England cost me one hundred fifty dollars," I said to the expert.

"No," said my wife. "That wasn't the table you brought from England. Joel broke the table you brought from England."

"Who is Joel?" the insurance broker wanted to know.

Before I could reply, my wife said: "He's our son. He breaks everything."

"He doesn't break everything," I said angrily.

"You said so yourself last night," my wife said. "And what he doesn't break, Connie and Jennifer break." She turned to the insurance agent and explained: "Connie and Jennifer are our daughters."

The insurance man made a note which I was sure, read: "Three children—break everything."

I was so nervous I tried to light a cigar. "Where are the matches?" I said angrily.

"Joel was playing with them," my wife said. "If I've told him once I've told him a hundred times not to play with matches."

The insurance broker took out his pad and pencil. "Your son plays with matches."

"All the time," my wife said. "Do you have children?"

The broker said he did.

"Then you must know how children are."

I tried to change the conversation. "Now that sofa over there is worth three hundred dollars."

"It was," my wife said, "until Geneviève—that's our cleaning woman—ruined it with cleaning fluid. You see, the children got chocolate all over it and I told Geneviève to clean it, but she got the cheapest fluid, and I told my husband we should sue the cleaning fluid company, but he said to forget it."

The home-furnishing man crossed out $300 and put $98 in its place.

"You have a nice piece of African sculpture there," the expert said. I had it marked down for $450.

"You mean we did have," my wife said. "I knocked it down a few months ago, but I found this marvelous glue and put it together. Even my husband didn't know I dropped it."

"You could have fooled me," the expert said as he crossed out the $450.

By the time the inventory was taken, everything on my list had been cut in half.

But even that wasn't enough for my helpful wife. As the men were leaving she said to them: "I'm very happy you could come and I'm delighted we're being insured, because this is a very old house and the water pipes keep breaking all the time and our biggest fear has not been robbery or fire, but water damage."

"Old pipes, you say?" the insurance broker said.

"Just awful," she replied pleasantly. "You know how these Paris apartments are."

The insurance man made a notation in his notebook and both men left.

After they were gone I tried to pull myself together, but it was very hard.

"They were so nice and sympathetic," my wife said.

"Of course they were," I shouted, "but you forgot to tell them I smoke in bed."

"Why?" she asked. "Would that have been important?"

Leaving Your Children Behind

MORE and more people are traveling all the time. Therefore it follows that more and more people are finding it increasingly difficult to explain to the children they are leaving behind why the parents are going. How can you explain to a seven-year-old that the reason his mommy and daddy are going on a trip is to get away from him?

The following dialogue could take place in anybody's home. It just happened to take place in mine, and that is why I was able to write it down.

The scene is the bedroom, half-filled valises all over the floor, and the mommy and daddy are trying to get packed before the children walk in. But they fail, and suddenly a seven-year-old boy and a six-year-old girl and a five-year-old girl walk into the room.

"What are you doing?" the seven-year-old asks.

The daddy looks at the mommy waiting for her to speak. The mommy looks at the daddy, waiting for him to speak.

Silence.

"Why are you putting clothes in the valise?" the six-year-old demands while the five-year-old starts taking them out.

The mommy speaks first. "Your daddy has to go on a business trip and I'm going with him."

The seven-year-old demands, "Where?"

"To Corsica," the daddy says. "We'll only be gone a few days."

"I want to go too," the seven-year-old says.

'I want to go too," the six-year-old says.

The five-year-old, who is still pulling the clothes out of the valise, says, "Me too."

"You can't go," the mommy tells them, "because this is a very important trip and no children are allowed."

"Then why is mommy taking her bathing suit?" the seven-year-old demands.

The daddy says: "Because she may have to go to the beach with some of the wives of the people I'm going to see."

"Then why are you taking your bathing suit?"

"Because I may have to go with the husbands. What are you asking so many stupid questions for?"

Tears start welling up in the eyes of the seven-year-old, followed by tears welling up in the eyes of the six-year-old, followed by tears in the eyes of the five-year-old.

"Now you've done it," the mommy says to the daddy. "Why did you have to lose your temper?"

"Well, what's he trying to put us on the spot for? We're taking a couple of bathing suits with us, so already we're abandoning them to the ASPCA."

All three start howling.

"Now you've really done it," the mommy says.

"Okay, okay," the daddy says. "Shut up, everybody, and hear this. When mommy and daddy come back they will bring each one a present."

The howling begins to subside.

"What?" the seven-year-old wants to know.

"A surprise," the daddy says.

"How big?" the six-year-old wants to know.

The daddy holds up his hands to show them the size.

The howling starts again.

The daddy moves his hands out further. The howling continues. It continues until his arms are outstretched and almost thrown out of their sockets.

They finally calm down.

"When are you coming back?" the seven-year-old wants to know.

"In a few days," the mommy says.

"When is that?"

"On Saturday."

"When is that?"

"It's the day after Friday," the daddy says. "What difference does it make? You don't know the days of the week anyway."

The howling starts again. "I don't want mommy to go," the seven-year-old cries.

"I don't want mommy to go," the six-year-old says. "I want daddy to go but not mommy."

The five-year-old cries, "I want Kay (the nurse) to go."

The children are finally led out of the room to play with their toys while the mommy and daddy finish their packing. The money is given to the nurse, instructions to the cook and several friends have promised to look in every day.

The moment of truth arrives.

The daddy and mommy go into the living room carrying their bags.

The mommy says bravely: "Well, children, we're off."

No one looks up from his toys.

The father says nervously: "We're going. Isn't anyone going to kiss us good-by?"

No one says anything.

The mommy says desperately: "We'll be back in no time."

The daddy adds: "Tomorrow. We may even be back tomorrow."

They pretend they don't hear.

The mommy says: "I'm not going."

The daddy says: "Come on. This vacation was your idea."

Tears start welling up in the eyes of the mommy.

Downstairs, as the mommy and daddy get into the taxi, three little heads pop out of the window and one little seven-year-old voice shouts, "Don't forget the surprise."

Cat on a Hot Tin Something

UNACCUSTOMED as I am to use this space for classified advertisements, I wish to announce there is one two-month-old cat available *absolutely free* to any cat fancier who will take him.

I was asked to make this announcement by my son, who told me as soon as I got home: "Antonio says his mother is going to kill his cat unless we take him."

Antonio is my son's best friend, aged seven. He is known not only to his friends, but also to his father and mother as "the Tiger." Not since Clemenceau was called "the Tiger" has the name fitted anyone so well.

When my son broke the news about Antonio's cat I was visibly shaken.

"We can't take the cat," I told him. "The landlady won't let us have a cat."

"Well," my son said accusingly, "if we don't take him, Tiger's mother is going to kill it and it will be your fault."

"If Tiger's mother is going to kill his cat," I argued, "it's her fault."

"No," he argued, "Tiger said if we take the cat his mother won't kill it, so it's not her fault, it's yours."

"I'm sorry, but we can't take the cat."

"Well," our son said, "Tiger is going to call at seven o'clock and you better tell him, because I don't want to."

"Why doesn't his nurse give the cat to someone?"

"She can't," my son replied, "because she's in the hospital."

"Why is she in the hospital?"

"Because Tiger kicked her in the back of the leg."

At seven o'clock sharp the phone rang and it came as no surprise to me to find Antonio on the other end.

He didn't pause for formalities. "Are you going to take my cat?" he demanded.

"We can't take the cat, Tiger. Our landlady won't let us."

"Did Joel tell you if you didn't take the cat my mother would kill it?"

"Yes, he did," I said.

"And? . . ."

"We still can't take it. Look, Tiger, why don't you give it to a café. All French cafés have cats."

"No," he said. "He'd jump over everything and break the glasses and bottles. He broke my mother's best vase last week, and he knocked over a lamp yesterday, and today he scratched a table, and my mother says she's going to kill it."

"Tell me, Tiger, just out of curiosity, how did you get the cat?"

"A boy gave it to me. His mother didn't want him to have it."

"I have an idea," I said. "Why don't you just take it downstairs and put it out on the street?"

"No," Antonio said. "If I did that he'd run away."

"I see your point," I agreed. "Well, why don't you call Cora (a mutual friend of Joel's and Antonio's) and tell her if she doesn't take the cat, your mother will kill it."

"I did," Antonio said, "and Cora's mother said it was all right with her."

"To take the cat?"

"No," Antonio said. "To kill it."

"Well, I'm sorry I can't do anything for you, Tiger. You know how landladies are."

The Tiger then asked to speak to my son, and after their conversation Joel angrily told everyone I refused to take Antonio's cat.

I am now known throughout the entire household as "the Cat-Killer" and nobody has spoken to me since.

Yellow Rose of Texas

(In April 1961, France almost had a revolution and these four articles were written at the time.)

I WENT down to the American Embassy Monday morning to be evacuated but no one would have me. I explained to the girl at the desk I was writing a book called "First Train Out of Paris," and therefore wanted to leave immediately, but she said the embassy was advising no one to leave and had no intention of evacuating anyone.

"What is your name?" she asked me.

"I'm usually known as the Yellow Rose of Texas."

"Well, Mr. Rose," she said, "at this moment your American Embassy feels you have nothing to worry about."

"Nothing to worry about?" I repeated.

"You must remain calm."

"Remain calm!"

"Stay away from crowds."

"I must stay away from crowds."

"And you must remember this is strictly a French internal affair."

"That's well put," I said. "Strictly a French internal affair. Doesn't seem to be any reason for me to worry, does there?"

"Not if you carry your American passport."

"I have it right here next to my traveler's checks. There isn't any special evacuation plan for Diners' Club members is there?"

"Not that we know of," the girl said.

"I was afraid of that. Let me ask you something. In case of serious trouble how will you notify the Americans?"

"We don't anticipate at this moment any serious trouble."

"Of course not. That's a stupid question."

"But if there is any trouble we will notify you by mail."

"That's a good idea," I said. "There's nothing like a letter when things are going bad."

There didn't seem to be much more to wait around for so I left. At the Place de la Concorde I ran into a very excitable American friend.

"Have you heard anything?"

"Yes. I've just been fully briefed by a high official in the American Embassy."

"For heaven's sakes, what did he say?"

"It was a she, but she told me everything in strictest confidence."

"What did she tell you? I won't breathe it to a soul."

"Well, first she told me it was a French internal affair."

"No kidding?"

"She said I must remain calm, stay away from crowds, and carry my passport at all times."

"Is that all? Did she say it was safe for Americans?"

"Yes, particularly those who have a mailbox."

Four Sleepless Nights

I CAN hardly wait for the year 1980 when I gather all my grandchildren around me and say: "Did I ever tell you about the night when the paratroopers almost landed on your grandfather?"

Yes, it was a wild, sleepless four nights for those of us who live in the City of Light, and now that the threat of civil war is over I'm prepared to sell the diary I kept during the troubles.

Saturday, April 22– Received word of paratroopers taking over Algiers. Called wife to lay in supply of sugar just in case. Tourists called up and asked whether they should stay or leave. I urged them to leave. Easiest way I ever had of getting rid of visiting firemen.

Sunday, April 23– Went to movies with son and we discussed paratroopers landing in our neighborhood next to the Parc Monceau. My son assured me paras could never land in Parc Monceau, as it is absolutely forbidden for anyone to land on grass, and besides the gardiens of the parc were not only armed with pistols but also with whistles. He was most reassuring until Premier Debré went on air late Sunday night to inform the French population that paratroopers might be landing on Paris and to urge everyone to be ready for them.

Premier Debré told Paris populace that as soon as they heard the air-raid siren they should go by car or by foot to meet the misled paratroopers (many from the French Foreign Legion) and tell them of the mistake they were making.

Called up a friend and asked him if he had any intention of meeting the Foreign Legionnaires and talking to them. "What's the use?" he said. "I don't speak German."

Monday, April 24— My wife's dressmakers started calling in to pledge their fidelity to her in the crisis, assured her they were backing her to the limit, and asked her was there any chance of her paying up in case they had to leave France in a hurry.

Went down to Crillon Bar in hopes of picking up inside information from embassy sources. Met one of top men, but before I could ask him anything, he asked me: "What do you think will happen tonight?" Not much help there.

Only good news of day was no one was trying to break any windows at the American Embassy, the first time in years American windowpanes were safe.

Received call at four in afternoon from visiting firemen who said a taxi driver in front of their hotel offered to drive them to Switzerland immediately for $500. Did I think this was excessive? Looked up taxi tariffs for army coups d'état and found price was in line. Urged them to go.

Monday night went down to Grand Palais, where French had asked for volunteers for a people's army to defend France. Frenchmen from all walks of life, many of them prosperous middle-aged businessmen, showed up and fought to get into uniform.

Met one business acquaintance who said it was very inspiring and he had met many buddies he hadn't seen since World War II.

"What did you talk about?" I asked.

He shrugged his shoulders. "Business."

*Tuesday, April 25—*Parc Monceau still safe, according to my son. But everything else uncertain.

Everyone still scared silly. Can hardly eat sugar.

But then afternoon paper *France-soir* came out on stand with following headlines: "The American Secret Service Believes the Rebels May Possibly Attack the Mainland in Five Days." The story came from the *France-soir* correspondent in Washington, quoting CIA sources.

On the basis of previous CIA estimates, we all knew for certain the army rebels were finished. France had been saved!

Old Buses Never Die

IF THE taxis of the Marne saved France in World War I, the autobuses of Paris saved France in 1961. The army insurrection of April 22 is still being hashed over in Paris and in all the excitement no one has given credit to the role played by the retired buses of Paris, which were called up at an hour's notice on Sunday night to repel the paratroopers.

In France's greatest moment of danger, Premier Debré mobilized the French buses to drive out the would-be invaders.

It is to their credit that although many of them broke down and shuddered, when the call came not one bus refused to go out into the streets, even though many of them knew they would never come back.

An eyewitness who was at the retired-bus depot near the Porte de St. Cloud told me he happened to be there on Sunday night when the buses were called up. He said it was one of the most dramatic scenes he had ever viewed in Paris.

Many of the buses, twenty and thirty years old, were awakened from a sound sleep by a klaxon. They could hardly open their headlights when the inspector general of the bus-transportation system strode into the chilly barn that had been turned into an old bus home.

"Mes Vieux," he said to the buses, "France is in danger, and you are being mobilized to save her."

Old 83, which used to shuttle between Porte de Champerret and Place d'Italie, coughed nervously.

Old 91 shed a drop of oil and a weary 73 leaned heavily on 95.

"I know what you're thinking. Why can't the younger buses go?" the inspector general said. "Well, the answer is we need the younger buses to carry volunteers to their posts. You buses have been selected for far more dangerous works. Some of you will be driven out to the airports and stationed on runways so the paratroop planes can't land."

Old 85, which had been painted yellow, screeched in agony.

All the other buses stared in embarrassment.

"Other buses will be stationed near the bridges of the Seine," the inspector general said. "When the siren sounds we will take the air out of your tires and you will act as a barricade against the paratroopers."

Several buses shifted from first into second.

One of the buses in the back stripped its gears in anguish.

"If the rebels have tanks, you will throw yourselves in front of them to stop them from driving on the city."

There was an uproar in the barn as the buses let out their exhausts.

"I'd like a little quiet," the inspector general shouted. "We will give you each enough gas to get to your destinations, but don't try to roll away because if you do, I'll brake every one of you."

Several of the buses started to perspire grease, and one bus got sick and threw up all its antifreeze.

"Autobus Français," the inspector general said, "this is your finest hour.

"General de Gaulle expects every vehicle to do his duty. Let it be written in the omnibuses of history that because of you the Fifth Republic was saved."

All the buses straightened up proudly and with their indicator arms saluted smartly and roared out into the night.

Everyone knows the rest of the story—the story which bears out the saying that "old buses never die; they just make barricades."

She Dyed for Us

FOR months or even years the French will be debating why the generals' *Putsch* failed. Some say it was because the navy fired at Mers-el-Kebir, others say it was because the French air force pilots refused to fly the paratroopers to France. But I have my own theory: the rebels failed to grab any communication installations in the capital.

By that I don't mean the radio and television stations, which were well guarded, but the Paris beauty shops, where most of the news in France is disseminated.

Had the ultras taken over Alexandre's, Carita's, Elizabeth Arden's, and Helena Rubinstein's, they could have caused confusion in the entire country and sent everyone diving for the Metros.

I know this because all the hard news I could get on the rebellion came from my wife, through her hairdresser. Every afternoon I waited for her outside Alexandre's, where, while ostensibly getting her hair set, she picked up all the latest information, not only from the hairdressers, but also from the other clients, who were in constant touch with their cooks and chauffeurs.

All the coiffeurs in Paris without exception had remained loyal to General de Gaulle, and therefore we should count on the news to be accurate as well as up-to-the-minute.

What surprised me during my waits was the lack of protection the coiffeurs had. While tanks and Garde Mobile units guarded the key spots in the city, no one thought to put up barricades in front of any of the hairdressing establishments, which have the most powerful broadcasting centers in the country.

On Monday afternoon my wife heard from her taxi driver that the paratroopers in Pau were reported to be moving toward Paris. We immediately packed all our bags and rushed her down to Alexandre's to confirm if the rumor was true. While I waited with the children and luggage on the Rue du Faubourg St. Honoré, she went in to have a permanent. She came down three hours later, looking very beautiful, to inform me that the woman under the next hair dryer said her concierge told her it wasn't true.

Relieved, we took the children back to the house, but because my wife had gone to so much trouble, I had to take her to Maxim's.

Tuesday my wife heard, while having a manicure, that there was going to be a mustard shortage in Paris. This was not a rumor, but had been officially announced by the pedicurist, who got it from the chief stylist. My wife urged me to go down to Fauchon's and lay in a supply of mustard right away.

Not wanting to panic and look foolish, I first went over to Elizabeth Arden's on the Place Vendôme, which is just as accurate as Alexandre's but broadcasts on a different wave length. I discovered that my wife thought the pedicurist had said "moutarde" (mustard) when in fact the shortage was expected in "boutargue" (dried fish eggs). Therefore we are now the proud owners of ten cases of dried fish eggs, which during a siege, could be worth their weight in gold.

Alexandre was getting suspicious of my wife going in so much, and there wasn't much more they could do with her hair, so I suggested the only thing left was for her to have her hair dyed.

She agreed to this only after I pointed out the children's safety was at stake. And it's lucky she did because next to her, also having her hair dyed, was the wife of a Minister.

The Minister's wife had heard from her gardener that there was going to be gas rationing. This checked out with something a friend of ours, who had been to Helena Rubinstein, had told her husband. When my wife called to tell me the news, I immediately rushed out and bought fifty jerrycans of gasoline. It was only after they were delivered to the house that I remembered we don't own a car.

2. La Vie Politique

If You're a Woman--Don't Vote

THE story of the Bull Moose Party is one of the great stories of American politics, and I think it should be told again. (I told it in the July 1960 issue of *Harper's Bazaar*, but I kept the book rights.)

It was started because it was discovered that although the American woman had more in the way of material comfort than ever before, she was, according to all the experts, discontented with her lot.

Although many experts had been called in and millions of dollars in research had been spent to find out why American women were unhappy (mostly by aspirin companies who wanted to keep it that way), it was only last year that a group of selfless, nonpartisan, distinguished Americans were able to get to the root of the problem.

All seven of us, happily married men, were worried about our unhappily married wives. Our wives were the best-clothed, best-fed, best-loved American women that any of us knew, and yet lurking down inside them was a "discontent syndrome." Where had we, as American men and husbands, failed?

We began by discarding all the usual reasons an American wife gives her husband for her unhappiness, such as "You never talk to me at night," "You never want to do *anything*," and "All I seem to be running around here is a hotel." Then we threw out such red herrings as "lack of fulfillment," "drudgery in the home," and "undependable diaper service."

After several weeks of elimination, we finally hit on the American woman's main problem. She has the right to vote!

In the pre-Nineteenth-Amendment era, the American

woman was placid, sheltered, and sure of her role in American society. She left all the political decisions to her husband and he in turn left all the family decisions to her. Today a woman has to make both the family and the political decisions and it's too much for her.

It was so obvious to us that American women were incapable of voting and also fulfilling their functions as wives, that we wondered why no one had thought of it before.

There was only one thing to do. We had to work for the repeal of the Nineteenth Amendment.

We knew we could count on the support of every man in the United States, but because women had gotten into the habit of voting, we foresaw a certain amount of resistance from some fanatic females who couldn't realize we were really trying to help them.

It was determined that an official organization had to be formed and funds raised to get the campaign under way.

After much discussion we decided to call the organization "The Bull Moose Party" in memory of those wonderful days when women thought a voting booth was a place to change their bathing suits.

Mr. Robert Jones, an advertising art director and one of the great experimental printers in the United States, was ordered to start printing posters to be distributed all over the country.

His first one is considered a masterpiece in political circles. It said:

THESE ARE THE FACTS!

WOMEN CAN'T COOK
(96.4% of all professional chefs are men)

WOMEN CAN'T SEW
(89.3% of all couturiers are men)

WOMEN CAN'T EVEN HAVE BABIES
WITHOUT HELP
(92.7% of all babies are delivered by men)

If they can't do the things
they're supposed to do

WHY SHOULD THEY HAVE THE VOTE?

THE BULL MOOSE PARTY
dedicated in perpetuity
to the repeal of the 19th Amendment

The Bull Moose Is Man's Best Friend

Other posters pointing out "Votes Are Like Mustaches—FOR MEN ONLY" also had their effect.

But while the reaction to these posters, particularly in YMCAs, was terrific, it was felt by some members that an appeal to reason should at least be tried on the American women.

Jones went back to his printing press and came up with this one, which is considered one of the most reasonable posters in American politics.

> To the Ladies (God Bless 'Em . . . This is your fight too. A fight for glamour, a fight for romance. A *fight for you* . . . The Bull Moose Party thinks you're wonderful. Too wonderful to stand in line on Election Day. Too wonderful—yes, and too lovely—to vote . . . The 19th Amendment made a voter out of you. The Bull Moose Party will make a woman out of you. (And remember—a woman can make a man vote *her way*.) STOP THE ROT!

We asked the League of Women Voters to distribute this poster for us, but they refused, and several of our members were arrested trying to stick them up in women's locker rooms in country clubs.

But the impact of the message hit home and while it is too early to know the outcome, the Bull Moose Party feels that the coming elections will show the results of its work.

You are probably saying right now: "What can I, as a woman, do to help?"

The answer to this highly sensible question is: Stay away from the polls in November. Go to the hairdresser on Election Day and look beautiful when your husband comes home from casting his ballot. Show him you love him by trusting his judgment. After all, if he doesn't know who the President of the United States should be—who does?

Gastro~Disarmament

WHEN General de Gaulle was in Quebec he was treated, among other things, to a lunch of hors d'oeuvres, white birds, sea gulls, wild duck, and an ice cream sculptured like the Arc de Triomphe. In the evening at a banquet he was served a sea-food dish consisting of everything from lobster to cod tongue, followed by a specially prepared partridge, iced champagne sherbet, glazed pheasant, iced maple-syrup souf-flé, topped off with bonbons and assorted French fruits.

In Toronto waiting for him was a banquet starting with cantaloupe filled with strawberries, a new fish dish created for General de Gaulle, consisting of a boat-shaped puff pastry filled with a trout filet, mousseline sauce, and truffles, fol-lowed by leg of lamb, spring vegetables, stuffed tomatoes, asparagus, a salad in the shape of the Cross of Lorraine, and a mousse flavored with kirsch.

These meals served to an ally in time of peace were noth-ing compared to the lunches and dinners given to Premier Khrushchev when he visited France, nor to what Presi-dent Eisenhower was served in South America, nor to what Prime Minister Macmillan was given in Russia.

It is obvious that with all the heads of state visiting each other we're entering into an era of gastronomic diplomacy and instead of the world ending with a whimper or a bang, it could easily end with a burp.

In a state of peaceful coexistence it's going to be the man with the strongest stomach and not the strongest weapon who is going to come out on top.

Gastronomically speaking, the French are the strongest of the Big Four powers and are believed to have stockpiled 20-megaton rogons flambés (flaming kidneys), which can be delivered anywhere in the world by SAC (Super Alsacienne Chefs) in thirty minutes.

The Russians claim to have over one hundred ICMs (Intercontinental Caviar Missiles), which are now aimed at every banquet hall in the Western world.

The British are counting on their solid-fuel ICFs (Icelandic Cod Fish) and the Americans have surrounded the Iron Curtain with frozen foods and slow-moving surplus butter.

Gastronomic strategists have pointed out that the American are at a great disadvantage in the cold war, mainly because the President of the United States is on a diet, and the Russians know what he *isn't* supposed to eat.

Another disadvantage is that, by law, General de Gaulle is not permitted to give the Americans any culinary secrets and the Americans have protested that if they don't have their own bombe glacée they won't be considered a major power. Therefore the United States has decided, since the French won't help them, to test their own bombe glacée. A recent test on the ranges of the Hilton Hotel in El Paso brought strong protest from the Mexicans, who claimed they were affected by the fall-down. (One melted right into the Rio Grande River.)

The menus are getting stronger all the time, and it is expected that a Gastronomic Disarmament Conference will be called at Maxim's soon. On the agenda will be ways and methods of cutting down the number of diplomatic dinners and the courses served.

The West will propose eliminating the hors d'oeuvre as a starter and then, if that works out, the fish and meat courses. The Russians say they want to cut out eating altogether, but the West says this is impractical. At the same time the Russians will propose adding vodka to all banquets in place of wine. This, of course, is completely unacceptable to the French.

One of the reasons the United States won't agree on total gastro-disarmament is that the Russians will probably refuse to allow the West to inspect their kitchens. Anyone who has ever eaten in a Moscow restaurant knows why.

Even if they did allow inspections, American nutritionists have pointed out, the Russians could still set off small shashliks on swords underground.

It is doubtful that anything will come of the conference. Therefore, as we enter the new phase of diplomacy by eating, the United States would do well to support the President with the strongest liver, no matter what his religion may be.

A Report on Prestige

The Honorable Ed Murrow
United States Information Agency
Washington, D. C.

Dear Ed,

Congratulations on your appointment as director of the USIA. I'm sure you will find the work most interesting, and, while the pay isn't much, I understand it's a job where you can have lots of laughs, particularly when you appear in front of the Congressional committee in charge of authorizing USIA funds.

President Kennedy recently released two reports on our prestige abroad which were kept locked up in the USIA files during the recent Presidential election campaign by persons unknown, like President Eisenhower and Vice-President Nixon.

While the reports were good as far as they went, I am taking this opportunity of submitting a report on prestige abroad which I personally took at my own expense and refused to publish, as I was afraid it would tip the election in favor of Harold Stassen.

This is what I discovered:

More French people hate French people than hate Americans. I spent one evening at the height of the rush hour by the Place de la Concorde, and the things the French drivers called each other were worse than anything I have ever heard a French person call an American.

Contrary to popular opinion, Italians do not hate Americans who overtip. Ninety-three per cent of all Italian waiters said overtipping helps American prestige abroad, and 98 per cent of all hotel hall porters said if they had the choice between overtipping and Communism they would choose overtipping.

Although the Austrians thought we were lagging in the space race, the overwhelming majority, when asked where they would rather go first, Las Vegas or the moon, chose Las Vegas.

The West Germans on the whole said they liked Americans but didn't want to lend them any money. As one German put it: "Once you lend people money, they begin to hate you."

We found a certain amount of resentment in Israel toward Americans. As one kibbutz worker said: "The trouble with Americans is they're always trying to steal our atomic secrets."

American prestige in England has never been higher, thanks to the Ford Motor Company, which paid $300,-000,000 to buy out its British affiliate. As an underdeveloped country, Great Britain welcomes American technical aid and know-how, and is delighted to listen to Americans who are willing to tell how much better we do everything in the United States.

But we found the British divided on American GIs. Fifty per cent of the population said they liked GIs and 50 per cent said they didn't. The 50 per cent who said they did were women, and the 50 per cent who said they didn't were men.

When the Swiss were asked whether they liked Americans or not they all gave the same reply: "Our banking laws forbid us to give out any information on Americans, or any other nationality."

I guess that's about it, Ed. You can take it from there.

Yours for a stronger Voice of America.

A. B.

The Social Climber

WELL, it was bound to happen sooner or later: I was invited to the de Gaulles' the other night for a reception in honor of President John F. Kennedy and his lovely wife, Jacqueline. The invitation called for white tie and decorations, which is usually embarrassing for most Americans because they always have to rent both. But as far as I was concerned, no price was too great to pay for a reception of this magnitude, and I was as excited as a French general at his first court-martial.

Since my wife wasn't going (I've made it socially, but somehow she never has), she helped me get dressed and told me what to say when I met General de Gaulle and President Kennedy. What you apparently say is: "Mes respects, Monsieur le President" to General de Gaulle, and "Good evening, Mr. President" to President Kennedy. It seemed easy enough and I kept saying it over and over again in the taxi so I wouldn't forget.

It was raining like the devil and although I started off at 9:30 I was five blocks from the Champs Elysées in a long line of cars filled with people in white ties and decorations at 10:15, the hour the reception was supposed to start.

It looked so hopeless I decided to hop out of the cab and make a run for it. So did everyone else, and I found myself in a 1,000-meter steeplechase being paced by a woman in a long evening gown and a fur cape who had jumped out of the chauffeured car in front of me.

Fortunately her husband was carrying ten extra pounds of decorations and he floundered in the mud at the last hurdle, so I beat both of them to the door.

A member of the Palace Guard took my invitation and I was directed to the hat-check line, which was also five blocks long, though at least it was out of the rain. But I didn't mind waiting because it gave me a chance to rehearse my lines. "Mes respects, Monsieur le Président," "Good evening, Mr. President."

After I checked my coat I was told to go into a waiting room where I was joined by the cream of French society, including the Cyrus Sulzbergers, the Joseph Alsops, the Marquis Childses, the David Schoenbruns, and the Garde Républicaine.

Beautiful women who had been sitting at hairdressers' for weeks, and had paid hundreds of dollars for their gowns, were crushed against perspiring husbands in starched collars and soaked shoes squishy from the rain. All of us were bunched together like French asparagus, staring at each other's necks, waiting to move forward in what appeared to be the direction of the receiving line.

But the line hardly seemed to be moving. The men were fretting and the women were frothing.

By 11:30 I had advanced from the first waiting room into the second. Somewhere ahead I could hear faint sounds of music. It sounded like someone was having a reception, though you could not prove it by me.

Suddenly, at 11:40, the line broke and everyone rushed forward at once. The reason was that both General de Gaulle and President Kennedy decided to forget about the receiving line and go to bed.

By the time I got into the main hall where the orchestra had been playing, the liquor was cut off and the reception was declared officially over.

I had no choice but to turn around. The same group pushed slowly back toward the cloakroom to get their coats. An hour later I was back out in the street, the rain mixed with my tears, my shoes squishing as I kept mumbling to myself: "Mes respects, Monsieur le Président," and "Good evening, Mr. President," over and over again.

Help Wanted

WHENEVER I get a moment, I try to think of ways of help-
ing to ease the American balance-of-payments deficit. I've
offered my services to the Government as a dollar-a-year man,
but I've been turned down by the State Department because
they said they need the dollar.

So instead I've forgotten the profit motive and I am now
offering my services absolutely free.

The French franc is now one of the most stable currencies
in Europe, and there is full employment. As a matter of fact
there is a labor shortage, particularly among servants. What
would be wrong with sending Americans to France to work
as servants? They would work for francs and presumably
send a part of their salaries back to the United States to
their families.

But before coming, an American must decide what kind
of servant he or she wants to be.

There are several designations of servants in France. On
the lowest level is the bonne à tout faire, who is expected to
do everything—cook, clean, wash, iron, and take care of the
children. Because she has to do everything she gets the least
pay. In France, as in every civilized country, the more a
servant does the less she gets paid.

Next in line is the femme de chambre. She makes up the
bedrooms, does the ironing and mending, helps Madame get
dressed, and when Madame is not in the house she keeps
busy, running away from Monsieur.

Then there is the cuisinière, who does the cooking and is
in charge of the dining room. She very rarely gets chased
by Monsieur, because she has so many knives and saucepans
at her disposal.

There is always a fight between the femme de chambre
and the cuisinière over who cleans the salon. The femme de

chambre insists, since the guests take their coffee in the salon, it's part of the dining room and should be cleaned by the cuisinière. But the cuisinière says from her experience in a French household the salon is usually part of the bedroom.

To settle this argument, most French families take in a daily maid to clean the salon.

Then there is the gouvernante, who is in charge of the servants and also in charge of the linen and silver closets. She usually starts off as a femme de chambre and it's doubtful an American could come in and be a gouvernante right off the bat, though a girl with a degree from Smith College might be able to do it.

For American men there is the job of valet. The valet takes care of Monsieur's clothes, cleans all the shoes, drives the car, and, when Monsieur is not there, he is kept busy running away from Madame.

The valet is in a very difficult position because if he serves breakfast in the bedroom, and messes it up, the femme de chambre gets very annoyed, and if he serves dinner in the dining room and messes it up he gets hell from the cook.

The French will pay anything to get a good American valet, particularly if he's been a former Army officer.

The thing to remember as an American working for French families is: always be polite and keep in mind that you're a servant and should stay in your place.

You can discuss your employers' indiscretion with servants of other households, providing they discuss theirs with you.

When house guests discover that you're an American servant they will become curious and will probably ask you questions about the United States. Don't be afraid to tell them. It will probably mean a good tip.

While you can't do anything about your employers, if a house guest starts chasing you, you have every right to seek protection from the American Embassy.

Peace Corps Volunteer

PRESIDENT KENNEDY'S Peace Corps is now getting under way. As I understand it, the Peace Corps volunteers would go to underdeveloped countries, live and work with the people, and give them the benefit of skills that Americans have learned so well.

I'd like to volunteer for the Peace Corps if I could choose my own assignment. One of the most urgent areas requiring technical skills and help is the French Riviera. There are people on the Riviera walking around half naked, lacking shelter, and many still don't have their own yachts.

In the underdeveloped towns of Cannes, Nice, and Monte Carlo, long lines of unemployed and untrained people stand around roulette wheels and chemin de fer tables hoping for financial aid and the technical assistance that will give them a better way of life.

As a volunteer of the Peace Corps I would be willing to drop everything and go down to the Riviera to help them. I would live the way they do, eat the food they do, share their homes, and show them that an American is not too proud to become one of them, no matter what hardships he has to face.

I would be willing to instruct the Rothschilds in basic money problems, I could show Mr. Onassis how to build tankers cheaply out of plywood, and the Aga Khan how to use the sea as a source of food.

I would instruct the women how to make the most of their Diors and Balenciagas and how to develop their natural resources. With the latest American cosmetic equipment they could earn diamonds, pearls, rubies, and emeralds which they could eventually exchange for rice, meat, and other staples.

I could show the men how to plow with their Ferraris

and Mercedes, and how to handle their polo ponies so they could get the most out of their crops.

I would set up gin-rummy schools to take advantage of the local skills, and I would show the natives how to get twice as much use out of their water skis without having to use any more water.

The Riviera folk have been kicked around by everybody. They are very suspicious of anybody who wants to change their customs. They see nothing wrong in wearing bikinis in the daytime and black ties at night.

They show surprise when an outlander objects to their thrashing a servant because he served their soup cold, and they become hurt easily when they invite a girl to go for a cruise on their yacht and she refuses.

Yet, despite the fact that they cling to their old customs, I think that if I, as a member of the Peace Corps, could have just one summer with them on the Riviera, I could teach them the American way, and by living with them and showing them how we do things back home, they would be a happier and more contented people: It's worth a try, and it's better that we get to them before the Russians do.

Dogs of America, Arise!

I DON'T have any bones to pick with the Russians for sending two dogs and a man into space, but it's pretty discouraging to walk around Paris and look into the faces of French dogs who seem to be saying: "What happened to your American dogs?"

I got to talking at lunch with two American writers, Sid Dorfman and Danny Arnold, and they also were depressed about the Russian achievement.

"If Nixon had any class," Mr. Dorfman said, "he would have made his campaign slogan 'If I am elected I will send my dog Checkers to the moon.'"

Mr. Arnold said: "It's obvious American dogs are six months behind Russian dogs. The attitude of American dogs has been one of complacency."

Mr. Dorfman agreed. "All American dogs are interested in is creature comforts. They think they're doing enough if they tip over a garbage pail, retrieve a rubber ball, or chase a postman down the street. While they've been playing around, the Russian dogs have been studying calculus, chemistry, and astronomy. It's no wonder we're so far behind."

"I think the basic fault," Mr. Arnold said, "is that American hero worship of other dogs is not based on scholastic achievements but on the money a dog makes. Who does the American dog admire more than anybody else? Lassie. Lassie, as far as other American dogs are concerned, represents the easygoing, good-natured, lovable canine image—the All-American Dog."

"Americans spend millions of dollars on jeweled collars," Mr. Dorfman said, "and haircuts, and doghouses. But what do they spend on dog education?"

Mr. Arnold said: "American dogs are too soft. We keep them on leashes and we feed them vitamins and food out of cans."

Mr. Dorfman agreed. "In Russia a dog can only get fed when they ring a bell. Pavlov had the right idea. Don't feed 'em until they're drooling with saliva."

"The big mistake," Mr. Arnold said, "is we treat our dogs as pets. They don't know they've got a mission. The day a dog is born in Russia he knows he's part of the Soviet space program. And he knows if he doesn't come up to expectations he'll soon be pulling a sled in Siberia."

Both Mr. Arnold and Mr. Dorfman felt that as long as dogs in America think that all they have to do is amuse children they will never be ready for flights into space. They also felt far too much emphasis at dog shows was placed on looks and not brains.

Mr. Dorfman said: "I've never heard of a dog at the Madison Square Garden Dog Show getting a blue ribbon for being smart. Why don't the judges look at their heads instead of their hind legs?"

"Our dogs are so spoiled," Mr. Arnold added, "that they'll only get a dog to the moon if a man goes up first to be his friend."

Mr. Dorfman felt that now that the Russians had gotten their dogs up first, it might be dangerous for an American dog to go up in space. "I think each American dog that is sent up into space should be provided with 7,500 rubles in cash and a poison dog biscuit, in case he gets caught by a Russian dog."

"If the Russian dogs get to the moon first," said Mr. Arnold "I think we should fire our astronauts and start training some veterinarians."

"Yeh," said Mr. Dorfman, "and the way things are going, when a man finally gets to the moon the first words he'll have to utter are 'Down, boy, down.'"

The Missile Explained

IN THE now famous Air Force manual, withdrawn temporarily but not forgotten, one of the paragraphs aimed at Air Force Reservists said: "The idea that Americans have a right to know what is going on is foolish."

We poor, ignorant civilians can't be blamed, then, if we have to resort to conjecture about what is going on with such things as our missile program, which is no longer known as a missile program but a missile gap.

I was as confused about our missiles as anyone else until I had lunch the other day with an industrialist who explained it to me. He asked that his name not be mentioned, and since the Air Force won't tell me their secrets, I won't tell them mine.

"The trouble with most Americans," he said, "is that they think ideas for a new missile come from the top. On the contrary, most ideas for missiles are thought up by some $10,000-a-year civilian engineer in some tiny office thousands of miles from the Pentagon.

"Let me give you an example of how a missile is born. One day a civilian engineer has to think of something new, so he writes a paper suggesting we develop an anti-anti-missile missile.

"The civilian, after developing the paper at length, turns it over to a second lieutenant, just out of ROTC, who, knowing less than anyone, immediately signs it and passes it on. The captain over him adds his signature, because he also doesn't understand it and doesn't have enough reasons for rejecting it. The paper continues on up through channels with more and more signatures, each office signing it on the assumption the guys down below know what they're doing. This is what is known in government circles as 'management from the bottom up.'

"Finally it goes to the Pentagon, who assume the problem, on the basis of all the signatures, has been thoroughly studied, and they take it over to the Appropriations Committee, who appropriate the money because they don't understand it either and therefore can't say it won't work.

"Besides, all they need to get the missile started is $10,000,000, and as long as it's such a reasonable request no one wants to argue about it.

"As soon as the money is appropriated the public-relations people put out a release announcing their branch of the service will soon have an anti-anti-missile missile that, although not the final deterrent, will be the gap filler which everyone has been waiting for 'until we catch up with the Russians.'

"The program is under way now, and in no time at all the appropriations are used up. Nothing has come of the missile, but this is an advantage, not a disadvantage. The people in charge believe it is really an advanced idea, otherwise it would be working already. The reason it couldn't be done, according to the people in charge, is that there wasn't enough money. So appropriations are increased to

$75,000,000 and, whereas only a few hundred men were connected with the original work, thousands are now added, on the theory that if you put enough people on a project long enough, they will get the job done. This is known as 'snowing the job with manpower.'

"The only thing that has been working so far has been the mimeograph machines in the public-relations department, and they have promised the American people an anti-anti-missile missile come hell or high water. When the $75,000,000 is used up, it's no problem to get more money for the project, because as long as you keep asking for more money in the Defense Department no one is going to ask you what you did with the other money. But as soon as you stop asking for money you're admitting the project is no good. No one has the courage to stop the project after so much money has been expended.

"Finally the time comes when you have to test-fire your missile. It doesn't go off. But even this is not a defeat as far as the service goes. After the failure, a general is on tap to explain that it's really a good thing to have failures, because they represent progress. If it worked it would not be an advanced missile but an obsolete one. Anything that works in missiles is obsolete.

"Therefore, the general explains, the Russians, although they seem ahead in the missile race, are really behind, because their missiles work better than ours. Anyone knows a really advanced missile is one on paper that can't get off the ground.

"In the meantime, the engineer who thought up the idea has corrected his original figures. But it's too late. Who is going to listen to a $10,000-a-year civilian engineer when $200,000,000 has been poured into a project?"

Lovlost Finds Its Way

MANY people are still not too clear about what exactly is happening with the gold reserves in the United States. It appears from what President Kennedy has said, and what Secretary of the Treasury Douglas Dillon has tried to do, that the situation is serious.

Nothing could dramatize the plight better than what has happened in Lovlost-by-the-Sea, that tiny European country that has been a bulwark against Communism and friend of the United States since the early days of 1946.

As everyone knows, Lovlost was on the side of the Germans in World War II and was therefore entitled to immediate financial aid from the United States once the hostilities had ceased.

Since 1946 Americans have poured in $150,000,000, until today she has one of the strongest economies in Western Europe. Just before the Marshall Plan went into effect, Lovlost's currency, which is known as the "bardot," was one of the weakest in the world and it took five hundred bardots to make a dollar. Now it takes five hundred dollars to equal one bardot.

It is this strengthening of the bardot that has caused a drain on the United States gold reserves.

To make matters worse Lovlost is a vital link in the chain of Western European defenses, and it has the only carrier pigeon station in NATO.

While the bodies of the pigeons can be handled by Lovlost, only the beaks may be touched by the Americans. It is for this reason that American troops, a private and a corporal, have been stationed in Lovlost.

When President Eisenhower put out his edict that Army dependents had to come home, it raised a bitter fuss in Lovlost. The corporal, who had a wife with him, said nothing, as he was carrying on with a girl from Lovlost. But the private, who was unmarried, was furious, because he was in love with the corporal's wife.

The private protested to the Secretary of Defense, pointing out that if the corporal's wife was sent home, morale among the United States forces in Lovlost would go to hell. But while the Secretary was sympathetic, he said that no matter how noble the cause "no exceptions could be made."

The first step in America's dramatic effort to halt the flow of gold to Lovlost was made.

The next step was even more dramatic. The Army PX in Lovlost, one of the largest in Europe, with five hundred civilian employees, was forbidden to sell Scotch, Canadian whisky, or French champagne. Since the corporal drank beer, and the private made his own liquor from raisins, not too much of a saving was made there. But, as Pentagon officials explained, if the corporal was promoted to sergeant he "might" start drinking Scotch, and it was better to lock the barn door before the horse was stolen.

The third step was by far the most dramatic. The President decided to send the Assistant Secretary of State for Lovlost Affairs to plead with the Lovlost Prime Minister to pay for the costs of maintaining American troops in Lovlost.

In one of the worst slaps to American prestige the Prime Minister turned down the Assistant Secretary flat and said: "Thanks to American aid, the bardot is now the strongest currency in the world. If we helped share the military burden, the bardot would be weakened again and then we would have to ask for an increase in American dollar aid, something we don't want to do, as you yourself say the dollar is in trouble."

The only thing that came out of the Assistant Secretary's visit is that everyone in Lovlost started to panic and exchange dollars for Spanish pesetas.

But as the Assistant Secretary pointed out when he got home, "Lovlost is now aware of our situation and for that reason alone my trip was worth while."

The Numbers Game

THERE are so many different economic and military organizations in Paris these days that the only way to keep track of them is by numbers. The Fifteen, for example, refers to the North Atlantic Treaty Organization, the Eighteen is the OEEC. Then there is the Twenty-one, which is made up of the OEEC plus the United States, Canada, and a representative of the EEC. The Twenty-one originally was the Thirteen, a special committee set up to consider basic economic questions affecting Europe and North America, which was created in December 1959 and called into session in January 1960.

After meditating, meeting, and debating, the Thirteen adjourned and became the Twenty-one.

The Twenty-one has been meeting ever since, and sometimes they are meeting officially to try to decide the fate of the Outer Seven and the Inner Six. The Outer Seven was organized after the Inner Six organized *their* Common Market. The Inner Six, composed of France, Italy, Belgium, Germany, Holland, and Luxemburg, invited Great Britain at one time to join with them.

Britain refused and instead organized the Outer Seven, consisting of Denmark, Switzerland, Britain, Sweden, Norway, Austria, and Portugal.

Now the Twenty-one are trying to get the Inner Six and Outer Seven into some kind of agreement so they will become the Lucky Thirteen.

What makes the situation difficult is that in the Twenty-one are five countries who call themselves Les Oubliés (the forgotten)—Greece, Turkey, Iceland, Ireland, and Spain. The Forgotten Five haven't been invited to join either the Inner Six or the Outer Seven, and they feel they've been left out of things. So although they are trying to get the Six and

Seven together, they won't benefit by it, unless by some miracle the Lucky Thirteen becomes the Unforgotten Eighteen, which is highly unlikely at the moment.

In the meantime the United States, which stayed out of the original Eighteen (OEEC), is joining with Canada and the EEC in the Twenty-one, which will be known as the OECD, the Organization for Economic Co-operation and Development.

This, by the way, is the organization that Russia asked to join, but it was turned down because the other members considered Twenty-two a crowd.

When you get down into lower numbers you must not omit the Working Four, composed of the United States, Great Britain, France, and West Germany, which is concerned with the problems of Germany and Berlin.

It is not to be confused with the Big Three, which are also concerned with the problems of Germany. The Big Three is made up of the United States, Great Britain, and France. General de Gaulle would like to see the Big Three take over the directorship of NATO, as he feels they should be the leaders. But the United States feels that as far as NATO is concerned the Fifteen should all have an equal say.

One of the reasons General de Gaulle wants the Big Three to have more of a say in NATO is that he is suspicious of the English-speaking Two (the United States and Great Britain). There is, for example, the sharing of atomic secrets, which the English-speaking Two are participating in. This chumminess between the Two, General de Gaulle feels, weakens the Big Three.

For the moment the Big Three's main function is to meet in the Big Four with Russia. But since Russia refuses to meet with the Three, Russia is now known as the Grouchy One.

The important thing to remember is that all this adds up to Ninety-Five, which is my tip for today's lucky Lottery Ticket.

Guess Who's a Spy

THE following paragraph appeared in the anti-Soviet newsletter called *Soviet Survey*, which monitors Russian newspapers and magazines: "Art Buchwald, the *New York Herald Tribune* columnist, has become the favorite of Soviet editors in recent months; at least a dozen of his columns have been reprinted in the Soviet press, and one in particular, recommending that Kennedy's Peace Corps be sent to the Riviera, has been given wide publicity."

Now some people, not in the know, might think this is a bad thing and on the surface it looks like it is, particularly since the editors lift the stuff right out of the paper without permission and, what's worse, they don't pay for it.

But anyone who has had dealings with me knows how anti-Communistic I am. For one thing, my son is one of the founders of the John Birch Society in Paris.

For another thing, I'm so sensitive about Reds, Left Wingers, and fellow travelers that I once had my wife blackballed from the Screen Writers Guild when I discovered she saw *Song of Russia* during the war.

When I drove to Russia several years ago in a Chrysler Imperial, I kept painting U.S.S.R. GO HOME signs all over Czechoslovakia and Poland, which caused a great deal of embarrassment in high government circles.

But my greatest coup to date has been getting the Soviet press to use my articles.

Because what they don't know is that my column, which looks very innocent on the surface, is actually written in code and every fifth word is a secret message to one of our agents in the Soviet Union who read *Izvestia* and *Pravda* religiously for my columns now to get their instructions from Allen Dulles.

For example, the Kennedy Peace Corps column, which

was so widely disseminated in the Soviet Union and was even read on the Moscow radio, was in fact a code to our people there which said: "Find out when the Russians are going to send a man up in space."

Thanks to the Russian editors and radio people, the CIA was able to get the information a month in advance of the event, and when the Russians launched Gagarin in orbit, our intelligence people had all the information on the launching, which astonished other countries but came as no surprise to the United States.

Proof of this was that when the public relations officer for the American astronauts was awakened at three o'clock in the morning and asked for comment on the Russian event, he was quoted as saying: "If you want anything from us, you jerk, the answer is we're all asleep."

I can't reveal what the other messages said to our agents, which were disguised in my columns, as some of them are still being decoded, but all I can say is that having the Russians pick up my columns has been the most efficient and fastest method of contacting our people in the U.S.S.R. that the CIA has ever devised.

There is a very important message concerning Laos in this column and all I can hope and pray is that the editors of *Pravda* and *Izvestia* reprint it, because the sooner our people can decode it, the happier everyone in Washington will be.

3. Les Touristes Encore

Two Happy People

As SOMEONE who has made a close study of tourism (there must be a cure for it) I believe I have isolated a certain type of tourist that for some reason has become more prevalent in recent years. This is the type of tourist who hates traveling.

While I've written in the past about individual tourists who hated traveling, I have discovered a new type of tourist who needs somebody else to hate it with.

There are couples now traveling who know before they even leave the United States they're going to hate it. But no matter how bad they think it's going to be, the reality is even worse than their wildest nightmares.

I met a couple like that the other day. They had been touring Europe for a month and they were on the homestretch in Paris. When I caught up with them they couldn't decide which they hated more, Venice or Rome.

"Jane," the man said, "didn't like Rome, but I still thought it was better than Venice."

Jane said: "That's because Harry didn't have the experiences I had. I still maintain I'd rather spend four days in Venice than two in Rome."

"It was that bad, huh?"

Harry said: "Well, it wasn't as bad as Zurich."

Jane agreed: "We both hated Zurich. We didn't have any fun in Zurich at all. It was almost as bad as Copenhagen."

"You didn't like Copenhagen, huh?" I asked.

"Does *anyone* like Copenhagen?" Harry wanted to know. "Would you like to hear what happened to us in Copenhagen?"

"Not particularly," I said.

"We were terribly disappointed in Amsterdam," Jane said.

"Almost as disappointed as we were in Brussels," Harry said. "We couldn't wait till we got out of there and got to London."

"Which," said Jane, "turned out to be dreadful."

"The funny thing," said Harry, "I hated it, but I thought Jane liked it, so I said I liked it."

"And," said Jane, "I thought Harry liked it so I didn't tell him I hated it. You can imagine our surprise when we discovered we both hated it. If we had known it at the beginning we would have left right away."

"But where would you have gone?" I asked.

"Not to Monte Carlo, that's for sure," Harry said.

"I don't see what Princess Grace sees in *that place*," Jane said.

"You can have the entire Riviera as far as we're concerned," Harry added. "Just try to get a good dry martini on the Riviera. Just try."

"I know some good places where you can get a dry martini," I said.

"You've been living abroad so long," Harry said, "you don't know what a good dry martini is."

"Well, what about Paris?" I foolishly asked.

"The worst," said Jane. "The people are so unfriendly and the prices are high, and I don't see what there is that's so special about Paris."

"Jane and I hate it," Harry said.

"You two seem to hate the same things," I said.

"Well, we know what we don't like," Jane said.

Harry said: "Europe's overrated. But we're glad we came because now we can understand why other people don't like it either."

I left the couple on the Champs Elysées. Harry was explaining to Jane why he didn't like the Arc de Triomphe, and Jane was telling Harry why she didn't like the Place de la Concorde. You couldn't find two happier people.

Tourist Topping

ONE of the great sports played during the spring and summer months in Europe is tourist topping. Any number can play, and the object of the game is to top another tourist no matter what the opponent says. Mr. Jim Backus, the American television comedian and the voice of Mr. Magoo, the famed animated cartoon character, claims he's been playing the game since he arrived in Europe and he hasn't won yet.

"The trouble is," he said, "the tourist when he is away from home is basically a lonely man. He seeks out the companionship of people he would never see in a million years at home, and all he wants to do is talk about *his* trip. Unfortunately the people whom he seeks out also want to talk about *their* trips and this is where the art of tourist topping comes in. I have been basically handicapped by the fact I've never been abroad before. But I'm learning fast, and perhaps on my third or fourth trip I may be able to win a match or two."

I asked Mr. Backus how tourist topping was played.

"Well, take for example the other night. I was at the Tour d'Argent with my wife and at the next table was a farmer and his wife from Nevada. We got to talking and I casually mentioned that I had run the ship's pool on the *Queen Elizabeth* and Lady Docker won it two nights in a row. I said Lady Docker wanted to buy the *Queen Elizabeth* but the Cunard Company didn't want to break up a set. I thought that was pretty good and any farmer from Nevada would be impressed, but not this one.

"He said to me: 'The little lady and I have been down to Kenya. One day we were surrounded by three hundred baboons and then we were attacked by a rhinoceros.'"

Mr. Backus continued: "My wife, who is no help to me when I'm playing, said: 'What did you do?'"

"The man replied: 'What did I do? I went down to the American Embassy and asked them what the hell was going on around here.'"

"You lost?" I asked him.

"Three straight sets," Mr. Backus said.

"The next day I went into the bar at the George V. It was in the afternoon, and the only ones there were the bartender and a man on another stool sipping a Pimm's Cup.

"I started up a conversation with the man by saying: 'It's good to be on land again after being on the *Queen Elizabeth* for five days. I'll never forget the third night out when the sea started rolling and . . .'

"The man looked up from his drink and said: 'I know what you mean. I was on the *Andrea Doria.*'"

Mr. Backus said: "You can't go anywhere without being topped. My wife wasn't feeling well the other day, so I went to the drugstore around the corner from the hotel. I said to the druggist: 'My wife isn't feeling well and I was wondering . . .' An American standing next to me said: 'You think your wife isn't feeling well? You should see my wife.'

"'Is she sick to her stomach?' I asked him.

"'Sick to her stomach?' he said. 'She hasn't eaten a thing in three days.'"

Mr. Backus said: "I told him: 'My wife hasn't eaten anything in four days. She can't even keep a book on her stomach.'

"The man replied: 'Any fever?'

"'One hundred and two.'

"The man said: 'Hah, my wife has a hundred and three.'"

Mr. Backus said: "The druggist gave the nod to the other man."

Part of tourist topping, Mr. Backus explained, was to make the other party think that no matter where you are, it's nothing compared to where he has just come from.

"When we were in London we met tourists who said it was nothing compared to Paris. Now that we're in Paris everyone says it's nothing compared to Rome. I'm sure when we get to Rome people will say it's nothing compared to London.

"One of the major strategies of a tourist topper is to make sure his opponent isn't having a good time.

"Even my wife has been topping me on this trip. Last week I took a walk alone and when I got back to the hotel I said to her: 'Guess who I saw on the Champs Elysées today! Ingrid Bergman!'

"She said: 'That's nothing. I went over to the Galeries Lafayette to buy some gifts this morning and bumped into Nina Khrushchev.'"

Get Away From It All

"There's a lot to be said for traveling," Don McGuire, a television writer and director from Hollywood, told me the other day at Fouquet's in Paris. "And there's a lot to be said against it."

Mr. McGuire considers himself a two-time loser, as he's been to Europe twice.

"I came the first time because everyone said my wife and I ought to get away from it all."

"Why did you come the second time?"

"Because," he said, "when I got home from my first trip I had everyone rolling in the aisles telling them what a lousy time I had. I was the rage of every dinner party. Pretty soon I convinced myself I had had the greatest time of my life. Every horrible experience seemed, in retrospect, a wonderful incident that I wouldn't have missed for the world. Pretty soon I had it worked out in my mind that I must go back and have some more laughs. If I only had let well enough alone.

"It isn't Europe," Mr. McGuire said. "It's traveling with your wife that does it to you. Most American husbands don't know anything about their wives until they travel with them. Couples could go for years, happily married, adoring each other, and then suddenly they take a trip and wham, they say to each other, 'Who are you?'

"You see," he said, "when your wife is on a trip with you she has no one to talk to, and there are no other rooms in the house where you can escape to. You're *it* for six weeks. No marriage should be made to stand the test of such a trip."

Mr. McGuire continued: "I've made a list of some of the great unanswered questions of our time that every husband is asked when he travels with his wife."

"What are they?"

"The one that takes the prize is 'What do you *really* think?' Next in popularity is 'How do you *really* like it?' Then there are such questions as, 'Should I go back there again?' 'Is it too long?' 'Too short?' 'Do you think they look too much off?' 'What should I wear tonight?'

"No man in his right mind would answer all of these questions, because all his wife is looking for on a trip like this is an argument.

"When you get right down to it, what do a man and woman who have lived with each other for any length of time have to talk about when they're on a trip? At home the guy doesn't see his wife all day, so when he gets home in the evening he can tell her what he did that day and she can tell him what she did. By the time they get that out of their system they turn to *Gunsmoke* on the TV and there is no problem getting through the evening.

"But when you travel you've been with your old lady the whole day and you sure as hell don't want to discuss *that* with her in the evening.

"Have you ever tried to read a book when you're traveling with your wife? I think there should be a Pulitzer prize for a guy who can get past the first paragraph.

"And sleep! At home, when a husband gets tired he says, 'I'm going to sleep.' But when you're traveling you don't go to sleep until your wife's ready to go to sleep, and no woman is going to sleep until she's put up her hair. So you get maybe three hours of sleep a night if her portable hair dryer works. If it doesn't you might as well be prepared to stay up all night and keep her company."

"What's the answer?" I asked him.

"You have two choices," he said. "When you get to Lake Como, you can hire a rowboat and do a remake of *An American Tragedy,* or you can fake it and pretend you're having a wonderful time. I think I hold the faking record for an American husband. It was in Lucerne, Switzerland, three years ago and it rained for four days straight, and we couldn't leave the hotel room. To this day my wife still thinks I had a ball."

Bored in Paris, France

EVER since Don McGuire has been in Paris I hate to leave his side, because every time we pass the Eiffel Tower he keeps asking when is the best time of day to jump off.

Since Mrs. McGuire spends her time in antique shops, museums, and stores, McGuire really doesn't have much to do with himself, so he thinks up things to pass the time.

Just yesterday we passed an American Army truck parked outside one of the U.S. Army headquarters in Paris.

Two men were slouched in the cab and an MP was standing next to the truck.

McGuire stopped, took a pad and pencil out of his pocket, and started writing down the number of the truck.

The MP said: "May I help you, sir?"

"You certainly may," McGuire said. "Just tell those men to get their feet off the dashboard and sit there like true American soldiers."

"Yes sir!" the MP said. Then he turned to the men in the truck and told them to put their feet down.

"Sorry, Sarge," one of the men said as they straightened up.

"Who's in charge of this unit?" McGuire demanded.

The MP spelled out the name of the lieutenant and after McGuire wrote it down he said to the MP: "Stand at ease."

The MP saluted and McGuire turned and walked away.

"What do we do now?" I asked McGuire.

McGuire pursed his lips. "Air France."

"What about Air France?"

"Let's see what's going on over there."

We went over to Air France and McGuire went up to the counter and said he wanted to get his ticket checked. The girl gave him a number and asked him to sit down and wait until his number was called.

McGuire said: "I'm Professor McGuire and I've got a space program and I don't have time to wait because at 1430 hours we're blasting an element of structure and we're faced with a cloud formation that exists in the next twenty-four hours of pressure area."

The girl had a hasty talk with her superior and Mr. McGuire was asked if he wanted a limousine to take him to the airport immediately.

He said he'd have to check with the tracking station, but to keep the limousine ready and he would be in touch with them.

"You didn't even tell them where you wanted to go," I said to McGuire.

"They'll have to hold a place on every plane leaving today."

When we got out on the Champs Elysées we saw an American tourist taking a picture of the Arc de Triomphe.

McGuire went up to him and said: "May I see your passport, sir?"

The surprised tourist took out his passport and showed it to McGuire without hesitation.

McGuire leafed through it.

"Do you have permission to take a picture of this military structure?"

"But I didn't know you needed . . ."

"I have a good mind to confiscate your film. But if you promise not to show the picture to anyone I'll let you go."

McGuire handed the grateful tourist back his passport and said: "Now remember, always ask first."

It was time for lunch and McGuire expressed an interest in going to a restaurant that is usually impossible to get in without a reservation.

He called up the restaurant from the drugstore.

"This is Mr. McGuire," he said. "Has the Duke of Windsor reserved a table for us?"

There was a pause. "Well," McGuire said, "I guess he wanted me to reserve it instead. We'll be four, and, captain, no photographers."

We took a taxi to the restaurant and when we arrived McGuire asked if the duke had arrived yet. The captain said no.

"Well," he said after we were seated, "we'll start without him."

We both ate lunch and as we were leaving McGuire said: "When the duke comes, will you ask him to call his house?"

At this point I started steering McGuire toward the Eiffel Tower. If he didn't want to jump, I decided to push him!

A Tale of a Shirt

WHEN someone is going to Europe someone back home always asks him to "do a little favor" for him. Mr. Tony Martin, the singer, was in Paris with his wife, Cyd Charisse, who was appearing in a dance film that was made here with Moira Shearer, Zizi Jeanmaire, and Roland Petit. When a producer friend in Hollywood heard that Mr. Martin was coming over, he asked the singer if he would visit his shirt-maker in Paris and order some shirts for him.

He gave Mr. Martin a sample shirt to take with him. It would just be a simple matter, the producer said, of dropping the shirt off at the shirtmaker's and ordering two dozen.

Mr. Martin agreed and took the sample shirt with him.

But when he arrived in Paris a week later, there was a letter waiting for him from his friend.

It said:

> Dear Tony,
> On the shirt I gave you, I would like you to explain to the shirtmaker that I would like the monogram made the same way as on the sample shirt. On the white shirts make the monograms in red (the same shade of red as the sample shirt), black, gray, and blue—several of each color. On the colored shirts make the monograms a deeper shade of the same color the shirt is made of. The monograms are to be placed on the left breast.
>
> The monograms on the pleated shirts and the formal shirts should be set on the left-hand sleeve, using the same monogram as on the other shirts. Also tell him to put heavier lining in the cuffs.
>
> > Sincerely,
> > Bill

Mr. Martin went to the shirtmaker and gave the instructions as he was told to do. He thought he had washed his hands of the matter, until he received a second letter from his producer friend.

> Dear Tony,
> Thanks for taking care of the shirts for me. I just received a sample shirt from the shirtmaker and it fit perfectly.
>
> But after having it laundered, I found it does not fit properly and that the collar is just a little bit too large and it does not lay down flat—it seems to roll up, for some reason. When I tie my tie the collar comes right together and there is no room for the tie to lay properly—the edges overlap.
>
> Now what I've done is send you a shirt I had made by Sulka's on which I like the collar very much. Please tell them to use this collar as a guide in making up a sample collar. You will note I have moved the button over on this Sulka shirt from its original position and have placed a safety pin where the button had originally been placed, as the collar was just a little bit too big. You will have to have them trim the collar on the sample shirt by this amount; you cannot make it fit properly by just setting the button over, because it throws the collar off. The rest of the shirt is fine, Tony, and after they have redone the collar, I am

certain there will be no problems in regard to the other shirts I ordered.

There is one more thing. As long as I'm sending over the Sulka shirt, would you have them put on a new pair of cuffs for me? You can't ask my shirtmaker to do it, because he doesn't have the Sulka material.

Incidentally I decided to also order two pleated shirts, and with the Sulka shirt I'm sending the pleating I want. Tell them to take the pleating off the front of this shirt and use the lace front on the new shirt. Then have them make up another shirt with the same lace pleating.

I hate to bother you, but you can appreciate the spot I'm in if the shirts don't fit. Lay out the money for the shirts and I'll pay you when you get back. The Sulka shirt and the pleating are being sent air mail and you should have them about the same time you receive this letter. I want to order some shorts, but Don McGuire is coming over soon and he'll get these for me, so don't worry about them. Can't tell you how much I appreciate this, Tony.

Sincerely,
Bill

Mr. Martin says he's in a terrible spot. He'd like to follow his friend's instructions, but when he gets back to Hollywood he's going to wring the producer's neck, and he doesn't know how the shirts will fit then.

How To Lose Friends by Being Nice

BEING nice to people can get you into a lot of trouble.

About three months ago I was in Maxim's with two friends of mine, when a man at another table sent over his card and said he was a good friend of a friend of mine whom I'll call Bob.

Now Bob was a schoolboy chum of mine and one of my close friends in New York. Any friend of Bob's is automatically a friend of mine and I invited the man and his wife to share a glass of wine with me.

The man, whom I'll call Eddie Berle, and his wife seemed like perfectly nice people and spoke in glowing terms about my friend Bob and his wife Sue. It seems, so they said, that they lived right around the corner from each other on Long Island and their children played with Bob's children and the wives exchanged recipes, the husbands exchanged golf balls, and now everything was complete because they had met Bob's best friend in Paris.

I decided under these conditions I should throw a party for the Berles—after all it was the least I could do for Bob and Sue—and so I did, and invited over all my friends to meet them. Then we had a nice dinner and the Berles went home the next day. Mrs. Berle assured me she would call up Bob and Sue as soon as she got back.

I forgot all about the Berles until I went back to the United States to cover the elections. Then I called up Bob and Sue, but they kept avoiding me. Finally I went over to Bob's office and demanded to know what was wrong.

Bob was very embarrassed, "I'm not mad at you—Sue is."

"Why is Sue mad at me?"

"Because," Bob said, "you were nice to the Berles."

"But I thought they were friends of yours," I said.

Bob shook his head. "Mrs. Berle is Sue's worst enemy. They haven't talked in over a year, except for that one time when the Behles got back from Paris."

Bob held his hand over his eyes to try and block out the picture.

"What happened?"

"Mrs. Berle called up Sue the day after she got back and told her, thanks to you, they had the most wonderful time in Paris. Sue couldn't stand it and she screamed, 'You told them you were friends of ours!'

" 'Of course I did,' Mrs. Berle said sweetly. 'Aren't we?' Sue hung up in a raging fury. You see for years people have been asking us to let them look you up and we've always said no.

"Many of them were our dearest friends, but we didn't want to bother you. And finally when someone did look you up it turned out to be Sue's worst enemy in the whole wide world. And what's worse is that the Berles are now going all over town telling everyone what dear friends you are to them. Sue is absolutely sick."

"But," I said, "I didn't know. How was I to know?"

Bob replied: "I admit it wasn't your fault. After all, you didn't know. But when Sue was so upset I said the Berles probably exaggerated and they may have shaken hands with you in a restaurant or something. But then your letter arrived telling us about how you entertained the Berles and how you found them such fine people and hoped we could all get together when you got to New York. That was just too much for Sue. She never wants to see you again."

"But," I said, "I only wrote that letter to be nice, I couldn't care less about the Berles one way or another. We were just being nice to them for your sake."

"That's it," Bob said. "That's the part that Sue will never be able to understand."

A Man With No Juice

LIKE I've always said, my main job in Paris is not working for a newspaper, but booking people in hotels, making reservations for them in restaurants and night clubs, taking care of their air-line tickets, and acting as a guide. The column is just something I do in my spare time.

Occasionally people get annoyed if I slip up on a request, and I'm awfully careful to see it doesn't happen too often.

The other day I received a call from London from two Hollywood songwriters, Sammy Cahn and Jimmy Van Heusen.

Mr. Cahn was on the phone: "Look, baby, we're coming to Paris on Saturday and we don't have any hotel rooms.

What would you advise? We don't want to stay with the yokels."

"Then you better stay at the George V," I said, "because they don't even allow yokels in the lobby."

The reason I suggested the George V was that it was the only hotel in town that wasn't mad at me. Having made previous reservations for Americans who never showed up, I find that most hotel managers in Paris won't speak to me.

"Okay," Mr. Cahn said. "Get us two bedrooms and a sitting room."

"That might be tough because the hotels are pretty crowded now," I said.

"Well, use some juice," Mr. Cahn said. "Juice" is a Hollywood expression which means "influence," and I didn't want to admit I had very little juice in Paris after living here all these years, so I said: "You'll have the rooms."

I went over to see Monsieur Louis Colonelli, the manager of the Hotel George V, and explained the situation to him. He told me it was very difficult.

"But you don't understand," I said. "These are not just ordinary songwriters. They write songs for Bing Crosby and Frank Sinatra and Mitzi Gaynor. They're up for an Academy Award and if they don't get a suite they'll go back to Hollywood and tell everyone I have no juice."

"No what?"

"Never mind. Please, Monsieur Colonelli, give them a suite."

Monsieur Colonelli said he would do his best and the next day he announced with pleasure that he had moved an Arab prince down the hall, and he had the accommodations for my friends.

I immediately wired Cahn in London telling him that all was well and the "juice" had worked.

Then I rearranged my plans for the weekend so I could spend as much time with them as they would need me. After all, it isn't every day in the week that two Academy Award songwriters came to Paris, and I was pretty excited.

Early Saturday morning I went over to the George V and

took a seat in the lobby. Mr. Cahn didn't say when he was arriving, but I didn't want to miss him.

Monsieur Colonelli came in a little later and we talked about the hotel shortage in Paris and how everyone expects hotel managers to work miracles, and we had a few laughs together.

Around four in the afternoon I started to get a little nervous, but knowing how late songwriters stay up at night, I figured they probably caught a late plane.

Monsieur Colonelli went home at six, leaving instructions with his night manager about the suite.

I went home around nine.

The next day I called the hotel. Neither man had arrived.

"Would you like to speak to Monsieur Colonelli?" the receptionist asked.

"Not on your life," I said and hung up. The last bit of juice had been squeezed out of me.

But all was not lost, because on Monday both Mr. Cahn and Mr. Van Heusen showed up. A friend had made a reservation for them at the Hotel de la Trémoille and they were very happy.

They didn't mention anything about their reservation at the Hotel George V, and I thought it would be rude if I brought it up.

But during lunch Mr. Cahn said to me: "Say, you don't have any juice at the Excelsior Hotel in Rome, do you?"

"No," I said firmly. "None at all."

"That's strange," he said. "How long did you say you've been living here?"

A New Travel Game

TRAVELING can become very boring, unless you can invent some games to pass the time.

I was introduced to one by an English writer, Guy Elms, who lives in Rome. He claims the game was invented by Graham Greene at a sidewalk café on the Via Veneto. It's called "Hating People."

Mr. Elms explained the idea of the game to me. "You play it in any public place—a sidewalk café, a railroad station, a train, or at an air terminal, waiting for a plane.

"You select one person from a crowd, someone you don't know, and you start to hate him."

"I don't understand," I said.

"All right, we'll play a game now. Do you see that man over there? Let's hate him."

Mr. Elms pointed at a young man sitting several tables down, reading a newspaper.

"Look at him," Mr. Elms said. "The supercilious bastard. He doesn't read anything but the sports pages."

"He looks pretty innocent to me."

"Hah," said Mr. Elms. "He's a miserable wretch, a troublemaker, and probably a Red. Look at him. He's trying to get the waiter. Watch, he's waving his hand. Who does he think he is? There are other people waiting to be served too. He's going to order one cup of coffee and sit there all day. How cheap can you get?

"Now look at the way he's ogling the women. He's probably a sex maniac. I'll bet the police would like to get their hands on him. Now he's put the newspaper on another chair. He's the kind of person that litters up a beautiful city. Doesn't care about anybody but himself. Oh, how I hate types like that."

"He does look like a bad sort," I said.

"Bad sort?" Mr. Elms said furiously. "He's a filthy rotter. Look at him scratch his ear. He hasn't taken a bath in weeks."

As I was studying him, an old lady came up to the table and joined the man. He kissed her on both cheeks.

"There!" said Mr. Elms. "That's his game. He's a gigolo."

"No," I said. "It looks more like she's his mother."

"Maybe so," Elms grunted, "but it's typical of him. He makes his mother meet him on the Via Veneto, instead of going to her house. He's too important to visit her; she has to visit him. When I think of what his mother did to raise him and the sacrifices she made for him I get sick to my stomach."

I started getting angry too. "A man should have more respect for his mother," I agreed.

"Did you notice?" Mr. Elms said. "He hasn't even asked her what she wants to drink. She probably walked up from the bottom of the Spanish Steps, but do you think he cares? He's spoiled rotten."

"They don't make them any worse," I said.

Mr. Elms said: "Look, he's laughing, telling her a pack of lies. Can you imagine anyone laughing with his mother?"

"Or at her?" I snickered.

"Now the waiter is bringing his mother a drink. It looks like a Pernod," Mr. Elms said. "She's become an alcoholic because of him."

"Do you think he'll pay for it?" I asked.

"Not if he can help it," Mr. Elms said. "He'll probably think of some excuse and stick her with the check. After all, he's been doing it all his life."

A man stopped by at the table to say hello.

Mr. Elms became furious. "He doesn't even bother to introduce him to his mother. He's ashamed of her. Look at the rat. He's forgotten his mother completely."

"After all she did for him!" I said, slamming my glass on the table.

"He's inviting the fellow to sit down. Can you imagine introducing your mother to a type like that?"

"No," I said, boiling. "I have a good mind to go over and poke him in the nose."

Mr. Elms suddenly relaxed and seemed to lose interest in the whole thing. He said to me quietly: "Forget it. It's only a game."

The Check Grabbers

WE LIVE in a world in which the grabbing of a luncheon or a dinner check becomes more dangerous all the time. Modern society requires most people in urban areas to dine out with their friends and acquaintances, and everyone seems to be faced with the same problem: How to keep from grabbing the check without actually looking like you're doing it.

Recently two of the greatest fumblers in check-grabbing history had a match in Paris at the Tour d'Argent. One was Herb Caen, columnist for the *San Francisco Chronicle*. The other was this reporter, who up until Caen's arrival held the French check-fumbling title.

This is what we said and what went on in our minds.

The meal is finished—each man is trying to outsit the other. Finally the waiter brings the check without being asked.

BUCHWALD (making a feint toward the plate): Here, let me take it. (*He probably will, too. Everyone thinks I have an unlimited expense account.*)

CAEN (lifting his elbow slowly): No, let me take it, Art. I'll charge it to the *Chronicle*. (*He probably forgot I took him to lunch in San Francisco.*)

BUCHWALD: No, no, no. This is *my* dinner. After all you took me to lunch in San Francisco. (*I took him to dinner afterward, but I'm sure that's slipped his mind.*)

CAEN (making slight movement with his wrist): You must be driven crazy by visitors all year long. Please let me take it. (*Maybe I'm sounding too insistent.*)

BUCHWALD (stretching fingers outward): Sure, a lot of people come through. But this is different. After all, you're a friend. (*I better watch out or I will get stuck.*)

CAEN: Look, I'm loaded with francs. Let me spend them. (*He will, too.*)

BUCHWALD: You'll need all those francs and then some to pay

your hotel bill. *(He doesn't know that I know Air France is picking up his tab at the hotel.)*

CAEN: Don't worry about my hotel bill. I have plenty for that. *(He doesn't know that I know he knows Air France is picking up my hotel bill.)*

BUCHWALD (trying to work cramp out of his hand): This is absolutely ridiculous, Herb. I invited you to dinner and I insist on paying. *(I invited him to dinner after he called me up and asked me what I was doing tonight. What was I supposed to say, I was going to Liège?)*

CAEN (pretending he's trying to get a spot off his tie): If I thought you had to take me to dinner when I called you, I would never have called. *(The only reason I called in the first place was that if he heard I was in town and I didn't call he'd get sore.)*

BUCHWALD (getting a weak grip on the saucer): I have an idea. Let's split it down the middle. Fifty-fifty. *(I'll charge the whole thing to the* Tribune.*)*

CAEN: Good idea, right down the middle. *(It's better than getting stuck with the entire thing.)*

Both men try to read the bill nervously. Suddenly they both smile and breathe a sigh of relief. The bill says, "Your dinner is with the compliments of the owner—Claude Terrail."

BUCHWALD: Good old Claude. At least there are still people willing to pick up columnists' tabs. *(Terrail must be getting soft in the head.)*

CAEN: The press over here sure has power. I can't thank you enough. *(He knew it all the time. He just wanted me to sweat.)*

Stately Homes of Brooklyn

I'm happy to report now that Americans realize they must have foreign tourists visit the United States if they ever hope to balance the flow of gold, that they are getting into the spirit of the thing. I just received a letter from my Aunt Molly who lives in Brooklyn and it shows that people are taking President Kennedy seriously.

Dear Arthur,

Your Uncle Leo says I should write to you to get your advice about the foreign tourists who are expected to flood America soon. He says we shouldn't overlook the tourist business and it's good to get in the ground floor. What your Uncle Leo wants to become is another Thomas Cook and Son.

I told him why should we bother you when on our very doorstep we have everything a tourist wants. I said we should start a Stately Homes of Brooklyn, and open our homes to tourists like they do in England.

I told him any tourist would be willing to pay 80 cents (30 cents round trip on the subway and 50 cents for the tour) to see a real historical American manor with leaking faucets and an oil heater that's always going on the fritz.

But your Uncle Leo doesn't seem to have much sense of humor and he said: "Enough with the jokes. Write Arthur."

I said I had it all figured out. I could show the tourists where I do the washing and ironing every day, and our historical bedroom with its Early Gimbel furniture, and the dining-room table where history was made when your Uncle Leo's boss Mr. Zimmerman ate $5.00 worth of steak and then fired your Uncle Leo two weeks later. And I'm sure everyone would pay 50 cents just to see the living room where your Cousin Milton hasn't left the television set since 1953. And then if they want romance I can show them your Cousin Ethel's bed on which she cried all night because Princess Margaret couldn't marry Capt. Townsend. I'm telling you, when I think about it there isn't a room in the house that if the walls could talk . . .

But it's not just the house that people would be thrilled with, but the extensive grounds as well. There's our Louis Quinze garage with its period Edsel, and stately driveway where your Cousin Ira used to play stickball before he broke the cellar window which your Uncle Leo never fixed. And we don't lack for pomp and ceremony either. Every night at ten o'clock sharp in front of our house we have the Changing of the Guard, when the Green Hornet Gang parades down the street knocking out the streetlight bulbs.

There isn't a tourist who wouldn't be moved by the ceremony. I've been living here 20 years and it still gets me.

But the more I talked about my idea the madder your Uncle Leo got, so I finally said I'd write to you and find out if you had any better ideas. He's got a notion but he doesn't want to go ahead with it until he hears from you. He wants to know what kind of postcards foreign tourists will buy, and do you think they'd buy them even when they can get "Playboy" on the magazine stand?

I have to go now and clean my stately home. I never know when the Duke of Bedford is going to pay me a visit.

Your loving,
Aunt Molly.

The Shoeshine Ploy

AL CAPP, the cartoonist, was in London doing some television programs for ATV, and I got into a discussion with him on the new trend of Americans building American hotels in Europe, particularly in London.

Mr. Capp thought it was a very good thing—with some reservations. "I have no objection," he said, "to American billionaires building Taj Mahals to give food and shelter to the homeless rich of the world. But, having spent half my life in American hotels, I feel that certain American hotel customs will come along with them and Europeans should be prepared for them.

"For instance, getting your shoes shined in a London hotel can be a very stodgy affair. You simply leave them outside your hotel room at night and in the morning you will find them shined. There's certainly very little suspense in that.

"But if you want a real thrill, try leaving your shoes outside an American hotel room at night. The chances are you'll never find them again, and the chances are even the FBI will never find the secondhand-shoe mob that stole them.

"If you're staying at an American luxury hotel, one which provides you with the luxury of a combination receptionist and armed house detective, and you make the mistake of putting out your shoes in the evening, this is what will happen:

"Your door will be pounded vigorously, and there the house detective will be. He will fling your shoes back into the room and will give you an insulting but valuable lecture about being such an idiot as to leave valuable possessions unprotected from the type of clientele that roams the corridors of a luxury hotel.

"The way to get your shoes shined in an American luxury hotel is like this. You phone for the bellhop. The American bellhop is not to be confused with the English page. An English page is a small and guileless boy who springs to respectful attention and says: 'What can I do for you—sir?' An American bellhop is a sophisticated, world-weary, middle-aged executive with income-tax problems, who says: 'What's on your mind, Mac?'

"The fee for simply summoning one of these busy and wealthy men is fifty cents. You give him this just to appease him and take care of his valuable time to reach your room. Now you're even. You owe him nothing more, until you speak to him.

"Suppose you say to him: 'Any chance of getting these shoes shined?' You must look embarrassed when you ask the question, as it's obvious to him that you've forgotten your do-it-yourself shoe kit, and to this overburdened executive who doesn't have time to pamper the whim of a guest, certainly a guest he didn't invite, there is nothing as stupid as a man who would ask a bellhop if he could get his shoes shined.

"The reply to your ridiculous question is: 'Well, it will take time.'

"Your expected reply to his reply is to give him a dollar.

"Now this softens him, but it doesn't move him. He has not yet taken your shoes. You're still standing there holding them like a fool.

"He says: 'I'll bring them all the way down to the barber shop and see if the shine boy has a free appointment to do them. You didn't make an appointment, did you?'

"You're nonplussed and admit that the first you thought of it was when you called the bellhop.

"The bellhop looks at you with disgust. After all, the shoeshine boy in a luxury hotel is also a busy executive with income-tax problems, and he can't be expected to just drop his racing form because a guest did not first ascertain whether he could spare the time—or wants to—to shine a guest's shoes.

"You then give another dollar to the bellhop to give to the shoeshine boy. Now you're out two-fifty and you have no shoes.

"But there is a gold spot in this black picture which I have just painted. If for some reason the bootblack cannot shine your shoes and the bellhop brings them back—all is not lost. This is because every American luxury hotel is prepared for such a situation. They all have shoe stores right on the premises.

"By simply giving the bellhop your size and another dollar, he will go down to the shoe shop and buy a brand-new pair for you which, to save you bother, can be charged on the bill.

"You see, American luxury hotels, giving the service they do, do not make their profit on the rooms or the food. They all make it from selling shoes."

The Poor American

THE BRITISH in the past fifteen years have seen many types of Americans, from Graham Greene's quiet one to Bill Burdick's ugly one, but if the Bank of England keeps buying up American gold, the British are going to be faced with something entirely new in their experience—the poor American.

As one of the first poor Americans to arrive in London this year, I felt it my duty to warn the British that the rich, jolly, good-hearted spenders that they knew for so many years would soon be replaced with poverty-stricken, frugal, sad-faced tourists who were lucky to have the bus fare from London Airport into town.

When I arrived at customs with my battered piece of luggage tied together with a string the customs inspector asked to see my passport.

Instead I showed him a hole in the sole of my shoe.

"Oh," he said, "you're American."

I nodded sadly.

"Do you have anything to declare?" he demanded.

"Oh, would that I could," I said, choking with emotion.

"Do you have any gifts for English friends?"

"Gifts for English friends?" I said in anguish. "The only reason I came is in hopes my English friends might give me some gifts."

"Do you have any cigars or tobacco?"

"You're making fun of me now," I said. "After what Castro did to us, we're lucky to have the naval base at Guantánamo Bay."

"And what about firearms?" he demanded.

"Firearms?" I said bitterly. "All the firearms we had **we** sent to Laos, and where did that get us?"

"Would you mind opening your bag?" the customs inspector said.

"But you never asked me to open my bag before," I protested.

"That's true," he replied as he watched me undo the string. "But that's when you were rich. Obviously no one with money would try to smuggle anything. We only search the bags of Hungarian refugees, Jamaicans, and, this year, Americans."

The customs inspector searched the bag and when he only found a torn suit, a soiled shirt, and a clip-on bow tie he made a chalk mark on the bag and said:

"I hope you enjoy your stay."

"With what?" I asked, sobbing.

As I picked up my bag a porter rushed up and said: "Would you like a porter, sir?"

"You must be kidding," I laughed, as I started the ten-mile walk into town.

Well, I've been in London for a week and I'm happy to report that Londoners are very sympathetic to poor Americans. They haven't flashed their pounds in front of us, they don't brag about what a ten-shilling note will buy, and British soldiers have promised not to take advantage of American girls who will soon be attracted to them because they'll be so much better paid than American GIs.

I could sense a whole new spirit in the air, as if the English are trying to say: "You've had your fling, but we forgive you for it; let's have a drink and talk about the war."

Perhaps in the long run the gold shortage may work to an American's advantage. After all, the British are always for the underdog, and now that we've lost the space race, they can hardly expect us to tip.

Don't Offend the Help

JAMES MICHENER, the author of *Hawaii, Tales of the South Pacific*, and other books, writes to me from Seville:

"I have another one of those guidebooks which warns that waiters and maids will be offended if you tip them more than is customary.

"Since I haven't yet met one of those gentle souls, I wonder if you could please seek one out and instruct us as to *how* offended he is, by what percentage of each overtip?"

Mr. Michener has put his finger on a very serious problem: how can we keep from offending European help by overtipping them.

So at his suggestion I decided to interview a few offended hotel employees in Paris on this touchy subject.

In spite of the fact that most European help are offended at overtipping, very few of them will talk about it. But with my connections I was able to discuss it with employees in several key Paris places.

At the Ritz, in the employees' dining room I saw a chambermaid crying her eyes out, while several of the other maids tried to comfort her.

I went up to her. One of the chambermaids was saying: "It's all right, Josette. It's all right."

"What happened?" I asked.

One of the chambermaids said: "I'll tell you what happened, Monsieur. A vache of an American woman gave Josette a twenty-dollar tip and six pairs of nylon stockings."

Josette, when she heard the words, cried even harder.

"Maybe the American woman didn't know that the service was included in the hotel bill," I said.

"Didn't know?" the chambermaid spat out. "And what about poor Josette? What about her feelings? Doesn't she have any? This is the second time it's happened to her this week. How much can a woman stand?"

Josette calmed down a little and, between sobs, told her story: "The lady asked me to wash and iron her lingerie which I was happy to do. One night she was cold so I brought her a hot-water bottle; another time she asked me to sew an evening dress for her. Monsieur, I assure you I did all these things without hesitation. There was nothing I wouldn't do for that woman. And then what did she do when she left?" Josette broke down again. "She overtipped me!"

"Why didn't you give her the money back?" I asked.

"I tried to," Josette said. "But she thought I was doing it because it wasn't enough, so she gave me six pairs of nylons besides. I was so upset I ran out of the room. Oh, I'm so ashamed."

Everyone started giving me dirty looks so I left the dining room.

I went to another hotel to talk to the concierge, who admitted someone offended him at least four times a day during the tourist season.

"Just this morning a client, a man whom I have known for years, told me he couldn't get on a train to Cannes and asked me if I knew anyone who could do it. I made a few calls and managed to get him the best accommodations available. And what was my thanks? He gave me ten dollars. Five dollars would have been plenty for such a service, so you can imagine how I felt. I have pride, Monsieur, and I will not forget. The next time this person asks a service of me I will tell him to go to the devil and take his ten-dollar tips with him."

I found a taxi driver who said the reason he doesn't accept tourists as fares any more is that he had been offended once too often by being given a 25 per cent tip instead of the normal 10 to 15 per cent tip. "The French," he said, "are the only ones who have never offended me."

I made one last stop, at the Gare St. Lazare, where I talked to several uniformed baggage porters.

They were all disgusted. One man spoke for the rest: "It says right on our uniforms that the charge is fifty centimes a bag, but do you think anyone pays any attention to it? Hah! Sometimes, particularly on the boat trains, they give us 1.5o francs and 2 francs per bag. What do they think we are? Believe me, sir, it's making Communists of us all."

Less Than a Dollar a Day

CAN someone tour Europe on less than a dollar a day? Two ex-GIs have been trying it for the past two months and claim it's not only possible but it can be fun.

They are Rob Wilkinson, of Pompano Beach, Florida, and Liam Clarke, of Rochester, New York. Both men served in the Army in Germany as chaplain's assistants, and decided they wanted to see Europe before they went home. They also decided money wasn't going to stand in their way.

First they thought they would hitchhike around, but this didn't work because Wilkinson is six-foot-three.

"It wasn't that people were afraid of me," he said, "it was just that it was too hard to accommodate me in small European cars."

So the boys bought themselves a Lambretta scooter and, with Wilkinson driving and Clarke clinging to the saddlebags, they've already seen four countries and hope to see several more.

To live within their budget, they have assigned themselves a bread day, a fruit day, a cheese day, and a raw-vegetable day. They always buy themselves a hot meal on Sunday night. They sleep in their own tent unless they can find some new construction going on somewhere. Then they crawl in under a roof and spread out their sleeping bags.

Both men are inveterate sight-seers and are constantly joining tours.

"When we see a tourist bus," Clarke said, "we follow it

with our motor scooter. Then, when it pulls into a château or a church, we hop off the scooter and sneak in with the tour. If we're lucky it turns out to be an English-speaking tour. But anyway it's better than seeing the sights alone."

Wilkinson has given up smoking except for Friday and Saturday nights and he allows the luxury of one airmail letter a week to his family.

"I don't have to write to my girl any more," he said sadly, "because when I decided not to rush home after getting out of the Army, I never heard from her again."

Understandably, Wilkinson and Clarke can't have too many dates on a dollar per day. Once they were on a sight-seeing boat in Switzerland and met two charming Swiss girls. They also met an American who called himself Uncle Phil. When the boat docked Uncle Phil said: "Well, boys, you have to make the choice. Either take off with your girls or come to dinner with me." It was no contest. The boys went to dinner with Uncle Phil.

Luck was with them in Nice. They heard that a company was making a film there based on the story of Lafayette. They motor-scootered over to the location and Wilkinson was hired to play a surgeon operating on Lafayette's leg, a job that paid forty dollars a day for two days. Clarke was hired to play a wounded soldier in a hospital who is visited by George Washington. According to the script, Washington tells Clarke to keep his chin up and Clarke promises he will. For this, Clarke got sixty dollars.

"After that," said Wilkinson, "we really splurged and took out some girls to the movies—twice."

But back to the question: can someone tour Europe on less than a dollar a day? The answer is yes, but only because every time Wilkinson and Clarke tell an American what they're doing, the American takes pity on them and buys them a meal.

I Am Being Followed

FOR the past twelve years I have been followed by a man I have never met or even seen. This man, for some reason I still haven't figured out, is determined to see that no matter where I go, I don't get any sleep.

It doesn't make any difference how secret I keep my movements—he always manages to find out where I'm going and then he either gets the hotel room above me or next to me and goes to work.

At first I thought it was an accident when he appeared, but now I am sure he really has it in for me, though for the life of me I cannot figure out why.

In the meantime I've been accumulating bits and pieces of information on him, and I know quite a bit about him and his habits, which may eventually lead me to his identity.

For example, I know he wears a large-sized shoe, possibly a 10 or 11. I discovered this seven years ago when I stayed at the Savoy Hotel in London and he had the room above me. Every morning at two or three he came in and dropped his shoes heavily on the floor two or three times, to make sure I was awake.

I know he smokes a lot, because five years ago at the King David Hotel in Jerusalem he started coughing every night at midnight, and didn't stop until seven o'clock in the morning.

He always carries a hammer with him and every chance he gets he starts hammering nails into the wall, but if he gets the room above me, he prefers to hammer tacks into the carpet. Once in Geneva, during the Big Four conference, the only accommodation he could get was a room three floors above me, so he started hammering on a hot-water pipe.

He's a very sneaky person, and when I leave word with the telephone operator, after a particularly late night, that

I don't want any telephone calls, he calls up anyway and pretends he wants to speak to a person in another room.

I know he owns a dog because once when I was on the *Liberté* he had the dog bark during the entire voyage.

He always seems to have a great deal of money. Two years ago I was staying at the Hotel Drake in New York City, and he couldn't get in, so he bought a pneumatic drill and started drilling a hole in the street below my window at eight o'clock in the morning. Another time he bought a motor scooter in St.-Tropez and sent his eighteen-year-old son out to rev it up all night long.

Several times he's had friends in the United States call him long distance at 3:30 in the morning, and then he pretends he can't hear them and starts screaming at the top of his voice. Occasionally he turns up the volume of his radio until I start banging on the wall, which is his cue to start banging back.

The reason I am writing about him now is he's turned up in Cannes at the Carlton Hotel, and this time he's brought along his wife. They're in the next room and they've been fighting with each other ever since I got here. I don't know if it's an act or whether they really hate each other, but the language they use at three o'clock in the morning is something frightening to hear.

When he isn't screaming at his wife he's coughing in the bathroom.

But this time he's gone too far. If his wife doesn't do it first—I am going to kill him with my bare hands.

4. Paris

A Lesson in Wine

I HAD lunch with George Sumner, a wine importer from the United States, and I got around to discussing the problems American tourists face when approached by a French wine waiter.

While many American restaurants make their profits from cocktails, French restaurants make theirs on wine, and therefore the sommelier, next to the chef, is the key figure in a French eating establishment.

There is a certain sequence of events that takes place in a French restaurant, and while the veterans of French dining may find this old stuff, this course is for the newcomers who have yet to face their first wine steward.

When the tourist arrives at a Paris restaurant he is greeted by the maître d'hôtel, who wears either a white tie if the waiters are wearing black ties, or a black tie if the waiters are wearing white ones. As in England, you can always tell a man's status by his tie.

The maître takes you to your table and once you are seated the captain comes over with the menus. Now there is a possibility that you might want cocktails before ordering (if you order and then order cocktails, you will probably get both your meal and drinks at the same time, which is okay with many American tourists, but it doesn't sell any wine).

If you wish cocktails, the captain will call over the sommelier, who will reluctantly take the order. A sommelier doesn't like to serve cocktails. It's beneath his dignity, and he only does it because he's been told to by the owner, who doesn't care what people drink as long as they drink *something*.

Now you've ordered the meal and the big moment has

arrived. What wine should you drink with the meal? The sommelier appears. He is usually wearing a black cassock with a white shirt front. Most sommeliers are fairly old and rather pale from spending so much time in the cellar.

The sommelier is carrying a small book with him that looks like a Bible. It is the wine list; as far as the French are concerned, it is a Bible.

If you're an American he will usually keep the book under his arm, as he assumes you don't know anything about wine and will take his advice on anything he suggests.

If you're the host and want to save face, stretch out your hand for the book. But remember this. He who orders the wine in a French restaurant must pay the check, so don't talk to the sommelier if you intend to be a guest.

Study the wine list carefully, clucking now and then while turning the pages slowly. Obviously you don't know one wine from another, but it gives you time to stall. When you've finally read the book you can then turn to the sommelier and say: "What do you suggest?"

If he's an honest sommelier he'll suggest an honest wine, but if he's dishonest he'll rattle off a Château somewhere in Algeria.

You nod your head, give him back the Bible, and wait for your food. While you're waiting the sommelier will return and show you the bottle, which is usually covered with so much dust you can't read the label.

Don't comment about the dirt on the bottle. It can only mean one of two things. He is either serving you a great wine or the restaurant has a very dirty cellar.

Now he will open the bottle and pour a little into your glass. Don't yell that you've been shortchanged. He only wants you to taste the wine, as is your prerogative as a host. You look at the color, sniff a few times, and then sip it slowly. Then with all eyes focused on you, nod again, which is the signal for the sommelier to pour the wine into the other glasses.

The sommelier, if he does his job well, will keep the glasses filled and when the bottle is almost empty he will ask if you wish another one. You'd rather not, but there's always one snake in the crowd that orders cheese, so you probably will have to order another bottle.

If the second bottle isn't finished, do not ask if you can take it with you for your dog.

It is an unwritten rule in French restaurants that undrunk wine goes to the help for their breakfast.

There is only one more thing to do with the sommelier before you leave the restaurant, and that's to tip him. If you give him two francs (forty cents) he'll be very happy. If you give him five francs (one dollar) he'll be delirious, and if you give him ten francs (two dollars) you'll only bear out his original conviction that you don't know a damn thing about wine.

Going to a Paris Movie

GOING to the movies in Paris is a novel experience that few tourists ever participate in; as most of them say, and rightly so: "I didn't come to Paris to see a film."

So for these people I'd like to explain what it's like to see a picture in the French capital: for convenience's sake, on the Champs Elysées.

To begin with, the French people don't mind standing in line for a good film, and you can always tell what the best pictures in town are by the length of the line. The longest lines are usually in front of the theaters showing a picture that is forbidden to children under eighteen years of age.

The reason for this is that, although in many cases the picture is lousy, there is always one scene in it that their friends have told them not to miss, such as Brigitte Bardot taking a bath, or Jeanne Moreau taking a shower, or worse.

So you're standing in line in front of such a film and you finally get to the cashier's window and present a hundred-new-franc note (twenty dollars). The cashier, who is loaded down with all sorts of bills that you can see, says: "Don't you have any change?"

You say you don't.

She gets very annoyed and tells you if everyone gave her a hundred-franc note she would have no change left at all. In the meantime people behind are starting to mutter and push forward. Finally, after the cashier feels you have been given a severe enough lecture, she gives you a ticket and your change. The ticket taker takes it, tears it in half, and gives you a half back.

The first hurdle is passed. But waiting inside to pounce on you is an usherette, dressed like a guard in a women's prison. Usherettes in French cinemas must be tipped and heaven help you if you try to take a seat unescorted.

You give the woman fifty or a hundred centimes. If you come in during intermission, the house lights are on, and after she seats you, you can always change places and sit where you wanted to in the first place.

Once you are seated you must wait for the house lights to go off. This time is not wasted because, since France does not have commercial television, they make up for it by showing commercials in the movie theaters. Many times these commercials are better than the film.

One of the games theatergoers play is to guess what product the commercial will eventually advertise.

A girl and boy might be out in the Bois de Boulogne kissing each other and then the girl sits up and says: "Wait, we haven't had our yoghurt yet." Or Louis XVI might be shown very agitated in the Palace of Versailles and you only discover later that it's because someone stole his instant coffee. A mechanic may be working on a new sports car and then wash his hair with his favorite shampoo, or a policeman may stop a pretty girl for a traffic violation, but after he sees her legs he lets her go because she's wearing the right kind of nylons. All this makes waiting for the feature a pleasure.

After the commercials are over the house lights still are not dimmed because the usherettes now go up and down the aisles selling ice cream, candy, and bonbons. This takes fifteen minutes. Finally, when the last sale is made the house lights go out and the news goes on.

The news is usually a minute of General de Gaulle arriving or leaving a monument, a few seconds of a news story such as the Congo or Algeria, five minutes of bicycle races, and ten minutes devoted to a new power station that has just been opened in the Pyrenees by the French government.

Then there is a short, maybe two shorts, and, finally, the main feature. Until the main feature starts, the theater has been very quiet, but the appearance of the titles on the main feature is the signal for the usherettes to start talking to each other and the customers.

Now, as I said, there is usually just one scene in a French picture that everyone goes to the theater to see. The rest of the picture is dull and uninteresting. They've already gone swimming at midnight and finally the guy is in the bedroom with the girl and he knows and she knows and you know that in just a matter of seconds, just a matter of—when, suddenly, four people come down the aisle with the usherette leading them. She seats them in front of you, shining the flashlight in your eyes, and while they take off their coats and one of them digs in his pockets for the tip—it's too late. For as your eyes get adjusted to the screen again, all that's left of the scene is the girl crying on the bed and the guy stomping out and slamming the door.

A Beatnik Painter's Claim Check

I HAD a date in Paris with a San Francisco beatnik poet-artist, William Morris, but he never showed up. I didn't think anything about it, because many people who make dates with me never show up. But six weeks later Mr. Morris walked into the office and apologized for not keeping the appointment. It seems the reason he couldn't make it was that he had spent the last six weeks in jail.

I was naturally curious as to what Mr. Morris had been doing to get into the clink.

To understand the story you must understand that Mr. Morris is an artist. He paints big—some of his canvases are forty feet long. Once in the United States he had an exhibition consisting of only one painting, which took up the entire four sides of the gallery. He made a splash for himself in San Francisco when he painted a picture called "Custer's Last Stand" using a truck tire instead of a paintbrush. Mr. Morris has had his problems in the past and most of them have appeared in the newspapers.

But when Mr. Morris arrived in Paris he was ready to have an exhibition and, while he hoped to get a certain amount of space in the French press, he said he had no desire to achieve it by going to jail.

This, according to him, is what happened. He arrived in Paris with a rolled-up 8-by-8-foot painting called "Grass," named after the substance it was painted on. He had to check his painting as baggage through Air France. When he arrived at the airport he took his painting, but no one asked him for a claim check.

Upon his arrival on the Left Bank in Paris he revealed to two friends that he received his painting but still had a claim check for it. One of them insisted Morris needed a business manager, and said there was more money to be made from Air France than there was to be made from painting.

In a few hours they worked out their plan. The "manager" went back and demanded the painting for the claim check. Air France, which takes great pride in the handling of works of art, was horrified to discover it had lost a painting, and started an immediate search for it. At this point Morris still had the painting in his room—it was only later when things got hot that he destroyed it.

When Air France couldn't find it, Morris and his manager demanded that the air line make amends. A fair price for a Morris painting, they insisted, was twenty-five hundred dollars.

While Air France continued its frantic search, Morris had a falling out with his manager and decided the heck with the twenty-five-hundred-dollar claim—he would get what he could out of the deal. So he went to the legal department of Air France, where he was received with great courtesy and respect—after all, in France, when a man loses a painting it is sometimes worse than losing his wife. The lawyer for the company said they would do anything within reason.

Morris said he would like a set of paints which could only be purchased in the United States, some canvas, and canvas stretchers. He would also consider a small token payment of say a hundred dollars, and call the matter closed. Air France sent to the United States for the paints and canvas, which they air-freighted to Morris. Since Morris also wanted cash, they asked him if he wished the police to investigate the theft.

Morris couldn't think of any reason why he didn't want the police in on the case, and so he said it was okay with him. But the police started to question a few of the artist's friends and in no time one of them revealed the whole story.

Morris was then questioned and assured if he told all he would be let off with just a warning. Morris told all and was immediately sent to jail.

For several weeks he remained in the Santé Prison without any word of his future. The judge had assigned a lady lawyer to him who brought him candy, but claimed she couldn't understand his paintings.

Then Morris met an Australian in the Santé who happened to be there for writing a bad check to a Paris furrier in exchange for a mink coat he had bought for his boy friend. The Australian said he knew of a lawyer who admired modern art and would probably handle Morris's case for nothing.

And so after six weeks in jail, Morris's new lawyer managed to get him out on bail. Morris in the meantime hopes to have an exhibition. It must be said that Air France has behaved quite well throughout the affair and never even tried to recover the paints and canvases they had flown to Morris. In gratitude Morris is going to paint an 8-by-8-foot canvas which will consist of a series of bars looking very similar to those on a prison cell. He will title the painting "Claim Check."

Instant Masterpieces

IF YOU live in Paris you have to keep up on the latest trends in the arts. In this way you can keep track of the art market and make a killing in it. At least you could in the past. But now the latest thing in art is to make things that won't last.

Iris Clert, who runs a Left Bank gallery under her own name, for artists with new ideas, told me: "Many of the artists today are protesting against the future. Now that there is the atom bomb they've lost interest in immortality. The idea is to do something for the moment."

The school of action painters, of which Jackson Pollock was probably the grandfather, has moved on and now the act of painting is more important than the painting itself. There is also a great interest in the amount of time it takes to produce a work of art, and it seems the less time it takes to paint a masterpiece the more pride the artist takes in his work.

Among the more famous of the action painters is Georges Mathieu, who sometimes paints while riding a bicycle, other times in costume, and on occasion he will paint his entire show on the spot. Mathieu's paintings fetch very high prices. Once he had a show in New York that was completely sold out. He still had a day more to stay in New York, so he painted another show.

Another action painter, Kujawski, paints ten pictures at a time, and a German painter named Sondorborg, instead of giving titles to his paintings, marks down the time it took

him to paint them. His best time was fifteen minutes—his slowest time three-quarters of an hour.

A Greek artist named Tsingos probably holds the record and is noted for doing twenty paintings in an evening. But Miss Clert said: "Only two are masterpieces. The rest he had to throw away."

The artists living in Paris are constantly finding new ways to express themselves on canvas. Yves Kline has reached the zenith in his use of nude models. First he decorates his live nude model with paint and then asks her to press herself across the canvas. The impressions left by the model constitute the painting.

There are also new things going on in sculpture all the time, and it's hard to keep up with them. A Frenchman named César is earning a living by taking old cars and crushing them with giant presses. The results have been exhibited as sculpture and several museums have purchased them.

Junk, the stuff you throw away, rather than what some artists smoke, has also brought success to another sculptor named Arman. Monsieur Arman recently had an exhibit at the Clert Gallery in which different kinds of junk were placed in glass bowls—one work of art was a fishbowl filled with broken electric razors, another was filled with toy pistols, and a third old alarm clocks. One that never sold but is very beautiful, according to Miss Clert, is a bowl of false teeth. "The colors, pink and white," she said, "make a beautiful design."

To launch the exhibit Miss Clert ordered two truckloads of junk with which she filled her gallery to the ceiling. There was just enough room in the gallery for people to walk around and look at it. Monsieur Arman spent two nights rearranging the junk, which Miss Clert thought was a mistake. "It was much more beautiful," she told us, "just the way the junkmen had left it."

Among Miss Clert's favorites is an Italian artist named Fontana, who invented the "space movement." Instead of using paint, Fontana takes a knife and makes large incisions in the canvas. For cutting up a canvas Fontana gets as much as a thousand dollars a masterpiece.

Enrico Baj, another Italian, prefers to use cracked mirrors in his paintings. One of his most famous pictures was a portrait of a general on which he stuck real medals he had bought at the Flea Market.

Miss Clert has a sense of humor about her new wave of "artists." "They're all crazy," she said, "and while they're like the Dadaists, there is one basic difference. Dadaism was a movement against art and it didn't sell. These people can sell almost anything they do. Today to be nuts is to be commercial."

But there are limits even for Miss Clert. Recently a young fellow came in with a white balloon in a box and said he had invented "pneumatic sculpture" which could be sent through the mail.

Miss Clert asked him what made the balloon a work of art, and the young man said indignantly, "My breath."

It's All in the Crust

WHAT is the secret of French bread? This is the question that Mrs. Margaret Rudkin, president of Pepperidge Farm, the largest independent bakery in the United States, has been studying since she's been coming to Paris for the past thirty-seven years.

"The secret," Mrs. Rudkin said, "is the freshness of the crust. The French will go to the bakery three times a day to get fresh bread. Americans prefer to go once a week and keep their bread in the freezer. When you go mad over French bread, you're going mad over the crust, which has a wonderful rich flavor as well as terrific eye appeal. French bread holds its flavor because it is sold unsliced and stays fresh longer.

"In the United States we're not allowed to sell unwrapped bread, and for this reason we can't get the crispness in our bread that the French do. When bread is wrapped, the moisture in the package, which can't escape, softens the crust, and we can't ever hope to have our crusts as fresh.

"The other thing, I think, that makes French bread so good is the holes in it. Americans refuse to accept holes in their bread—the French seem to like the holes. I find even the holes in French bread taste good."

But Mrs. Rudkin said that if she could develop a bread with holes in it she thinks diet-conscious Americans might finally go for it. "Those who are worried about their weight could say they're eating holes and not bread, and those who feel there is not enough nourishment in the bread could fill the holes with peanut butter."

Mrs. Rudkin whetted my appetite to find out more about French bread.

I found out French bread is to the Frenchman what the umbrella is to the Englishman. It is carried at all times, rain or shine, and has many functions. You can hail a taxi with French bread, use it to tap someone on the back when you want to get off a bus or to get a cat off the vegetables, and wave it when General de Gaulle drives by.

There are many types of French bread. The very, very thin long loaf is called "la ficelle," which means "the thread." The ficelle is mostly crust with very little dough inside. It naturally breaks very easily. Because of its thinness the ends are very pointed, and it must be handled more like a rapier than a saber.

The ficelle is excellent for sticking out of the car window when you want to make a right turn, and for pointing out places of interest to foreigners.

The next size is "la baguette" (the stick), which is the most popular size. The baguette is carried like a rifle, the butt of the bread in the palm of your hand and the other end across the shoulder. When meeting your boss or your wife on the street you present arms, holding the loaf vertically in front of you six inches from the top and bottom. In cases where people have suffered ski accidents it can also be used as a cane.

It is bad form to twirl the baguette or swing it like a baseball bat in the street.

Shorter and thicker than the baguette is "le bâtard" (which means what you think it does). The bâtard is a cross between the baguette and the "pain fantaisie" (fancy bread, which isn't very fancy). The bâtard is excellent for political demonstrations and carrying late at night in case of attack.

The "gros pain," or big bread, is as long as the baguette and as thick as the bâtard. It is chiefly bought by large families, but, because it is so unwieldly, the mother sends all the children to buy it. They usually carry it home like a ladder.

The French bakers, unfortunately, have been trying to imitate American sliced bread, but because it serves no use other than to be eaten, sliced bread in France hasn't been very successful.

Say It Ain't So, Jean!

THE latest French rage in motion pictures is called "La Nouvelle Vague" (The New Wave). No one is quite sure what the Nouvelle Vague is, except that it is a school of movie-making done by very young directors (preferably between the ages of twenty-two and twenty-six) preferably in black and white and preferably on a shoestring. The subject matter can be very good, as in the case of *Quatre Cent Coups* (*Four Hundred Blows*) and very bad as in *A Bout de Souffle* (*Breathless*), which has been described by film critics as the *New* New Wave.

A Bout de Souffle stars Jean Seberg, who was burned at the stake in the soon-to-be-forgotten *Joan of Arc*. She plays, of all things, a young American girl who sells, of all things, the European Edition of the *New York Herald Tribune*.

No one is quite sure of the story, which seems to be one of the intentions of the director, Jean-Luc Godard. As far as I could tell, *Breathless* is about a nice boy who likes to steal cars. In stealing one car he kills a policeman. While the police are looking for him he takes up with this nice American kid, Miss Seberg, and, though it's hard to believe, they wind up in bed together. Then she discovers he killed a policeman. She doesn't get too disturbed about this because she's not sure whether she loves him or not. While she's deciding, she helps him steal a few cars on the side. When she decides she doesn't love him she denounces him to the police, on the theory, I could only assume, that if you're not nuts about a cop killer, you might as well turn him in and let him make his own bed.

Now I'm not taking issue here with Miss Seberg's performance, which is far better than anything she's done so far. But it's very hard for someone who works on the European Edition of the *New York Herald Tribune* to see one of "our girls," wearing the famed yellow *New York Herald Tribune* sweater, consorting with a wild thug.

Everyone who has ever been to Europe knows the girls who sell the European Edition of the *New York Herald Tribune* are true in heart and pure in body, and refuse to have truck with any man except the circulation manager of the paper. There have been cases of the girls taking off to the Riviera on the back of a motor scooter and forgetting to return their unsold copies of the paper, but these girls are in the minority, and once they are found out they are never allowed to wear the *Herald Tribune* colors again.

Where one questions the credibility of *Breathless* is that one can believe an American girl might take up with a French car thief, and one, by stretching one's imagination to the limit, might conceivably believe a girl selling the *Herald Tribune* could take up with such a person. But it is impossible to believe that an *American* girl selling the *Herald Tribune* would do such a thing.

In selecting our girls for this interesting work, the first

question we always ask them is: "Have you ever stolen a car?" If the answer is in the negative, then we ask them: "Are you now going with anyone who has ever stolen a car?" If they say no to this, then we ask them: "Are you now living with anyone who ever killed a policeman?" If they say no to this question, they automatically get the job.

So you can see how farfetched it is for Miss Seberg to do what she does in the picture (and she does do it), and have the audience accept it.

Not too long ago a Norwegian girl wearing one of the *Herald Tribune* sweaters was walking up the Champs Elysées when a Frenchman said the equivalent of "What a beautiful balcony." The Norwegian girl hauled off and slugged him and knocked him out. She came back to the office tearfully and told the circulation manager what had happened. Instead of getting angry he gave her twenty-five more papers and transferred her to the Opera District, one of the most lucrative territories in all of Paris.

The slogan of the *Herald Tribune* circulation department is "Virtue has its own rewards."

Quiet Please--Hospital Zone

SOME time ago I wrote about my secretary, Ursula, and the problems she had trying to get married. It seemed that because Ursula was Swiss and her fiancé French, the French government was making it very difficult for her to get the required permissions.

But Ursula is a determined girl and finally, after knocking down all the high hurdles the French functionaries put in her way, she did get married, and, as happens once in a while after such a move, Ursula was with child.

There is probably no country in the world that respects a pregnant woman more than France, and after all her trouble trying to get married the French government has done a complete about-face and has indicated it is delighted she is going to have a baby—a French baby, of course.

When Ursula went down to the town hall to declare her pregnancy, the same man who threw her out a year ago when she wanted to get married now smiled, stuck out his hand, and said: "Felicitations."

He then left his window and escorted her into the Social Security room, where somebody immediately brought her a chair.

Behind the counter, interviewing pregnant women, were five people instead of the two that a counter this size in a government office usually holds. All five employees smiled and talked very softly.

When Ursula went up to the counter and revealed she was pregnant the clerk said: "How wonderful! You must get a complete medical checkup, an X-ray, a Wasserman test, and a dental checkup. But do not be alarmed; the government pays for all of it, and you will also be given twenty-one dollars for being pregnant. We will send you advice and little slips of paper. When your doctor signs them you will get more money, and in your sixth month we will give you forty dollars and when the baby is born another twenty dollars."

Besides all the money, Ursula was informed she was also entitled to a carte de priorité. A priority card in France is given to war invalids, blind people, and pregnant women. It entitles Ursula to a seat on the subway and the right to get on a bus before anybody else. She doesn't have to stand in line in post offices, railroad stations, and automobile shows. Department stores also give priority to pregnant women so they won't get tired waiting.

She also has priority crossing a street, and French drivers must stop when they see her. This is only theoretical, because no pregnant woman has ever dared to use *this* priority.

Once Ursula has her child she can have her priority card renewed for six months, on the theory that she must still be tired and also that she is in a hurry to get back to her little baby.

Since the French are determined to increase their population, they have set up all kinds of safeguards to encourage women to have babies. One is that now that Ursula has declared to me officially that she is pregnant I cannot fire her. No employer can fire a pregnant woman.

By law I have to give her six weeks' maternity leave with pay before she has the baby and eight weeks after, and then I have to take her back whether I want to or not (I do).

The rights of the boss during a woman's pregnancy in France are kept to a minimum. If Ursula gets sick while I'm dictating to her she can go home and I still have to pay her. If she makes mistakes typing I must hold my tongue so as not to upset her or the baby, and if she comes in late I have to smile and think of France.

I was so upset by the responsibility of having a pregnant secretary that I went down to the Social Security office to make sure everything Ursula told me was true.

The chief of the bureau confirmed everything.

"Can't I even scream at her when I get mad?" I asked.

The woman behind the desk looked at me in horror and said: "You wouldn't dare!"

The Sea of Silence

I WAS trying to get some sleep at seven o'clock the other morning when somebody in the next building started hammering on the wall with a sledge hammer. It seemed a bit early for such nonsense, and so I got dressed and went next door to find out what was going on. What was going on was that a crew of workmen was tearing up a large apartment and was getting an early start to do it properly.

This, I felt, was certainly against French law, though I wasn't quite sure what French law was involved. So at nine o'clock I went down to the Prefecture of Police and requested to speak to the persons concerned with noise.

I was sent to several offices, but no one seemed to know
who was in charge. Finally, I wound up in an office where
the man in charge turned out to be quite friendly. He said
he was very happy I was taking an interest in the noise in
Paris because it was a problem.

"I'm not really interested in *all* noises in Paris," I said,
"but . . ."

He told me: "Ever since honking horns has been forbidden
in Paris, the Parisians have been very sensitive to noise.
Before, everyone was honking so hard they couldn't hear
any other noise and consequently nobody complained.

"But I assure you, Monsieur, we are making headway.
Look at February," he said, taking a sheaf of papers out of
his drawer. "In February we fined 366 people for honking
their horns in the daytime and 34 for honking at night.
Sixty-six people were fined for noisy exhausts on cars and
motorbikes, 51 for noisy braking, 24 truckdrivers were fined
for carrying noisy material such as tin cans and empty gasoline drums in the daytime, and 19 after dark. Seventeen
bistros and night clubs were caught making noise at night
and," he added with pride, "six people were fined for beating carpets outside official hours."

"But," I said, "I want to know about . . ."

The man continued: "In March we put out a new rule
forbidding the playing of transistor radios in public places
such as streets, parks, and public transportation. Transistor
radios are only allowed in cars and only if they don't bother
the people outside the car.

"Believe me, we are making progress. We now have trucks
going around Paris measuring noise. Of course, there are
some noises that are more difficult to detect than other
noises."

"What are those?" I asked, forgetting my own problem
for the moment.

"Well, people playing violins or pianos, which we refer
to as *bruit de jouissance,* or pleasure noise. We can't very
well take their instruments away from them, and there is
always the problem of people who earn their living giving

music or singing lessons. All we can do is limit the hours
these kinds of noises may be made."

"That's very nice," I said, "but I have these men working
with sledge hammers next to me at seven o'clock in the
morning and I was wondering what to do about it."

"But," he said, "we are not concerned with that type of
noise. You must go to the Minister of Public Construction."
I went to the Minister of Public Construction, who sent me
back to the police station, but to a different bureau. This was
called the Bureau of Co-ordination of Local Services.

Once again I was greeted kindly, and when I explained
the problem to an official, he said: "No one has the right to
make *any* noise, whatever time of day or night. If you hear
hammering in the morning you must call your local commissariat and they will send a policeman over to listen to the
noise. If the policeman thinks it is too much noise, he can
fine the workers.

"If they still make noise, he can increase the fine up to
thirty francs (six dollars). We do not want noise in Paris.
As a matter of fact, starting in 1962, there will be a law
put in force that all garbage pails in Paris must be noise-
less and have rubber bottoms. Be assured that you have
every right to complain." He shook my hand.

The next morning, the sledge-hammering started again.
I was just about to call our local commissariat when my
wife pointed out to me, "Suppose the policeman comes and
they're not hammering any more? We could be fined."

It was a point. So I decided to try something else. I went
next door in my bathrobe, and visited with the crew, which
consisted of three men.

We chatted about the work and then I asked who did the
actual sledge-hammering. One of the men admitted he did.
I gave him twenty francs (four dollars). Then I gave ten
francs (two dollars) to each one of his helpers.

"No hammering before nine o'clock?" I asked.

"No hammering before nine o'clock," they all agreed.

I went back to sleep filled with pride. I was probably the

first American to contribute substantially to the Paris anti-noise campaign.

Smoke in Your Eyes

THE French government has a special interest in its citizens' smoking tobacco, because in France the tobacco industry is a government monopoly and represents one of the major incomes to the country.

Therefore, to celebrate the four hundredth anniversary of the introduction of tobacco into France, the tobacco monopoly put on a show at UNESCO, and a festive affair it was.

As part of the celebration a sixteenth-century-type orchestra was in attendance and praises of tobacco were sung by actors of the Comédie Française, government officials, and members of the Académie Française.

The orchestra played "La Servante au Bon Tabac" and Victor Hugo's poem "My Pipe" was read. Other quotations were read, including a poem about military people and tobacco, which said: "The best companion of the soldier is tobacco. Generals ought to smoke big, serious-looking cigars, colonels pipes, lieutenants cigarettes, sergeants small, bitter cigars to remind them of the rough life they lead, and the enlisted privates should take snuff."

One poem warned: "Don't break anyone else's pipe, or your own. Therefore only lend your pipe to your best friends, consequently you will enjoy your pipe above everything else, except your wife, and that only very rarely."

The audience was treated to two films and then Monsieur Grimanelli, head of the French tobacco industry, made a speech, naturally in favor of tobacco.

It was a beautiful speech and everyone lit a cigarette after he was finished.

At this point Monsieur Grimanelli should have quit while

he was ahead, but instead he announced that the French
government was not only interested in selling tobacco, but
was also spending money on research to find out if tobacco
really harmed people, and to reassure all those who were
afraid he would introduce Professor Truhaut, of the phar-
maceutical staff of the University of Paris.

Everyone applauded politely and Monsieur Grimanelli
beamed.

Professor Truhaut started off by saying he smoked, but
only moderately, and he knew why. He said: "Tobacco is
a drug; it isn't as bad as opium, but it's still a drug. This is
proved by the fact that once you start smoking you can't
give it up and also you get accustomed to bigger and bigger
doses."

The professor then went on to say that nicotine was a
poison that could easily find its way into someone's blood.

As Monsieur Grimanelli and other members of the tobacco
industry sat in stunned silence, the professor told about his
cancer research experiments, all pointing to the fact that
the tar from cigarettes did cause cancer in rats, and those
who smoked lived shorter lives than those who didn't.

Almost everyone put out their cigarettes as Professor Truhaut continued.

He went on to say that filters (which the French tobacco
people have been pushing) did absolutely no good and the
best filter was the cigarette itself, which should be thrown
away after being two-thirds smoked. "The last bit of the
cigarette is the most harmful."

Monsieur Grimanelli started to look desperate. But the
professor, oblivious to his discomfort, continued.

He said that they were able to impregnate cigarette paper
and the tobacco to remove the danger of tar, "but no one
would be able to smoke the cigarettes, they would taste so
awful."

Monsieur Grimanelli seemed anxious for the professor to
finish his speech, but the professor wasn't finished yet. He
turned to the head of the tobacco monopoly and said: "I am
now appealing to you, dear Monsieur Grimanelli. We need

money for research. I know you give some, but we need very much more. So please keep giving so we can advance our research work a little more quickly."

Monsieur Grimanelli jumped up, thus indicating that as far as he was concerned the speech was over, and didn't smile as he shook the professor's hand.

After the rest of the ceremonies, which seemed to be carried on listlessly, champagne and petits fours were served. All the reporters were trying to find Professor Truhaut to ask him some more questions, but unfortunately he had disappeared.

To paraphrase an old Madison Avenue saying: "Where there's smoke someone's bound to get fired."

A Dog's Life in Paris

A DOG's life is not an easy one in Paris, particularly if the dog wants to live in the lap of luxury. Iago de Roc-Fort, a miniature schnauzer belonging to producer Darryl F. Zanuck out of a gift by Juliette Greco, lives with his master at the Hotel Plaza-Athénée, in Paris. The charge for Iago is twenty-five NF (five dollars) per day, which includes no meals.

This infuriates Iago, whose uncle, grand champion Rossel von Himmelburg, lives at the Ritz for half the price. Iago feels that the high tariff at the Plaza is levied against dogs to discourage them from taking up residence at the Plaza, a hotel which, in the main, caters to people. When Iago found out what his lodgings were costing, he became very irritable and started barking at the help. He insists he's never bitten anyone, but just tried to scare them into reducing the rates.

This has led to some very difficult situations. Iago claims one time when he barked at a maid she swacked him with a towel, and another time, when Mr. Zanuck was shaving, a waiter tried to kick him through the bedposts for a field goal.

Another person whom Iago claims gives him a great deal of trouble is a woman dressed in a black dress who apparently is the housekeeper. When Mr. Zanuck is out and Iago is trying to nap, she sneaks into the room and checks to see if he has done any damage to the rugs and the furniture. Iago hates spies of any sort and only the fact that there is a hotel shortage in Paris and he might find himself out on the street with Mr. Zanuck has prevented Iago from chewing a chunk of the housekeeper's ankle.

Although Paris is supposed to be famous for its love and respect of dogs, Iago feels there is a great deal of discrimination shown toward pedigreed dogs, particularly those of German descent. He recently went with Mr. Zanuck to the Bristol Hotel and was not even allowed into the lobby. This was doubly insulting, since the Bristol Hotel is where all the German diplomats stay.

Iago is very sensitive about his race. He has been in many situations where a French poodle has been received in a restaurant as an honored guest but he has been put in the men's cloakroom with wet umbrellas.

Iago doesn't know whether he gets this treatment because he's German or because he's a dog.

He pointed out that no miniature schnauzer has ever taken up arms against the French. His grandmother, grand champion Eureka de Roc-Fort claims the schnauzers have been antimilitaristic since the days when they were taught by the Germans to hunt wild game. If the schnauzers were unsuccessful they were whipped by uniformed grooms, and schnauzers have no use for uniforms of any kind.

Iago takes at least one of his meals at the Relais Plaza, a grillroom attached to the Plaza-Athénée. He dines there with Mr. Zanuck, and claims he only barks at agents and screen writers. This is no more than Mr. Zanuck does with the same people, and Iago doesn't understand why the management gets mad at him but not at Mr. Zanuck.

Iago seemed so unhappy about his situation I wondered out loud why he didn't move.

He doesn't want to move, it seems, because the Plaza-

Athénée is so well located and has many advantages. He finds the Rolls-Royces, Bentleys, and Cadillacs parked in front of the Plaza are great for sniffing. He also says he meets the most interesting people late at night when they go for a walk, many of them young ladies who are out walking without their dogs.

Iago also feels that while his uncle has an easier life at the Ritz, it is not necessarily more exciting. Having struck fear into the hearts of the employees at the Plaza, Iago finds his position in the hotel is getting stronger every day. If Mr. Zanuck's money holds out, Iago says it won't be long before he will have the employees so frightened they'll be seating him in the dining room and hotel guests in the cloakroom with the wet umbrellas.

"A Funny Thing Happened on the ..."

THE women's milliners are pushing hats this year, and they're pushing them hard. They've conspired with the top Paris hair stylists, who have agreed to cut women's hair short this year. Short hair, according to all the experts, means more women will wear hats.

To get their message over, the hat makers gave a dinner and fashion show at the Eiffel Tower Sunday night for the leading lights of the fashion world and fashion press, of which I consider myself an honorary member.

My original intention was to eat the dinner and beat it before the hat show. But the organizers must have found out about it because they had the show *before* the dinner.

I must say they were pretty wild hats, as hats go, and I got lots of chuckles out of the show. It's hard enough to keep a straight face when your wife comes home with a new hat, but when you see about a hundred at one time I challenge any man who isn't in the business to keep from doubling up with hysterics.

Well, there I was having the best time in the world when one of the American organizers came up to me and asked me how I liked it.

I thought I was being nice and I said, "It's a million laughs."

He became grim. "You're not going to write anything funny about this?" he asked.

"Well, I don't know. . . ."

The man said: "Now please don't write anything funny. You see, I think it would be funny, but you know a lot of milliners don't have a sense of humor and they wouldn't think it would be funny."

"That is a point," I agreed. "Something that would be funny to you and me wouldn't be funny to them?"

The man said "Exactly."

"But at the same time," I said, "something that might not be funny to you and me might be funny to them."

The man shook his head.

"But if I wrote something about the hats, I might inadvertently be funny, but they wouldn't think I was being funny even though you yourself thought it would be funny."

"That's it," the man said. "I'd rather you'd not write anything about the hats if you're going to be funny about them."

"Well, it would be hard to write about hats from a male's point of view without being funny about them."

The man looked as if he wasn't following me.

I said: "But if I didn't write anything about the hats, that might be funny to the milliners, but it wouldn't be funny to the editor, who told me to cover the show and be funny."

"Yes," he replied.

"You've put me in a very unfunny position," I told him. "But I can appreciate the spot you're in, and if I write anything about the hats I promise I won't be funny about them."

So I didn't write anything about the hats.

But fortunately I was saved the next morning because I received a call from a Mr. Zan Diamond, of a New York

advertising agency, who said he had a funny story to tell
me. I told him to come over right away.

Mr. Diamond, it turned out, was pushing silver and gold
fox furs.

"You can really make something funny out of this," he
said. "For fifteen years, silver foxes have been out of style
but they're coming back again this year."

I started giggling.

"The funny thing is the only man who believed in silver
foxes was Mr. Edward Fromm of Hamburg, Wisconsin."

"That's a funny name for a town," I said.

"Mr. Fromm was the only one who saved his herds when
the bottom dropped out of the silver fox market. Some days
Mr. Fromm had to give his own dinner to the foxes to keep
them from starving."

I was laughing out loud.

"But twenty-three years ago he got this mutation of a
gold fox. You see, the dream of everyone is to make a gold
fox from a silver fox. So through genetics they're now breed-
ing gold foxes."

I had to admit it was pretty funny.

"Now Fromm Brothers have cornered the golden fox fur
market and silver fox is coming back again strong after fifteen years. You can make something funny out of that, can't
you?"

When I stopped laughing I said: "It can't miss."

So there you have it. Some people think there is nothing
funny about hats and other people think there's something
funny about silver foxes. As I was saying to my wife just
the other day: "You never know where your laughs are going
to come from any more."

The Venus de Milo's Big Toe

A READER, Mr. A. A. Caffery, has asked me to find out something for him. He wants to know if the big toe on the Venus de Milo in the Louvre is her real toe or a substitute toe put on after World War I. Mr. Caffery has reason to suspect the Venus de Milo's toe is not hers.

When Mr. Caffery visited Paris in an air service unit, just after World War I, he said that the Yank soldiers were given tours of the Louvre. They were shown the Venus de Milo, but Mr. Caffery said, "Most of those guys didn't know de Milo from 'September Morn' or White Rock's 'Lady of the Lake.'

"One night, a few days after our trip to Paris, one of the yokels in the outfit tossed a dirty piece of crockery on a blanket where a dice session was under way. He asked: 'Any you guys know what this is?'

"Nobody guessed. So the boy said: 'That's the big toe off that old girl in the Louvre—the one without any arms.'

"He went on to relate how he had fallen behind the guided party and, when no one was looking, knocked off the toe with his jackknife."

Mr. Caffery has been bothered by the incident ever since. On one hand the man who claimed to have done it was the idiot of the unit, and could easily have been lying; on the other hand he was just stupid enough to do such a thing.

Years ago, when a friend of Mr. Caffery was going to Paris he was asked to check the toe of the Venus de Milo. The friend reported the Venus de Milo had all her toes, and the war buddy was talking through his hat.

But Mr. Caffery isn't so sure. He believes the big toe on the Venus de Milo is a replacement job. Two recent visits to the Louvre have convinced him that his Yank buddy really did steal the big toe.

Mr. Caffery can't rest until he finds out the truth, but he may have to wait a long time.

A telephone call to the Louvre produced the following results. First, they denied they had ever heard of the Venus de Milo. Then they denied she was in the Louvre. Finally, they admitted having such a statue but it was impossible to tell me whether her big toe was her own or out of some modern twentieth-century marble quarry. It seems that the Louvre has a rule that all the dossiers on their treasures must be kept locked up for fifty years, and none of the contents in them revealed before then. Therefore the secret of the big toe will remain a secret until January 1, 1968.

But if it proves that his buddy did knock off her toe, Mr. Caffery feels a search should be made for his friend and on his death he should be stuffed and placed in the Smithsonian Institution as a very early example of what might be one of our greatest ugly Americans.

A Journey Through Paris

DURING a few days last year, Paris went through a series of what are known as "flash strikes." Different Metro and bus lines went on strike at different hours, causing monumental traffic jams throughout the city.

I didn't realize how serious it was until I had to go to the Tour d'Argent for a cocktail party in honor of Abel Green, the editor of *Variety*. The Tour d'Argent, located on the Seine, behind Notre Dame, is only two miles from the Parc Monceau, where I live, and so I felt I should travel light.

There were four of us in the taxi, not counting the taxi driver, and we took with us four liters of water, a loaf of French bread, some cans of fruit, and a carton of cigarettes. I figured this would last us until we got to the Tour, where we could replenish our supplies for the trip back.

We all started off in high spirits and the driver predicted we would be at the Tour d'Argent in three hours, Paris traffic being what it is at seven o'clock at night.

The first few blocks were easy, and it looked like it would be a piece of cake. The weather was clear, and even I was optimistic. But having made the trip before on a June evening, I warned everyone to go easy on the water. Yet the couple I was with had little experience in Paris traffic, and I noticed them sneaking sips from the liters when they thought I wasn't looking.

The first sign of trouble came as we tried to approach the Rue Royale.

First we moved slowly. Finally we came to a complete halt. We smoked three packs of cigarettes waiting for the light to change at the Madeleine.

The couple I was with had finished all their water and started eying my bottles, but, knowing what lay ahead, I refused to part with any.

An hour later, we were trying to cross the Place de la Concorde, but we bogged down by the Obelisk in the center of the Place. No traffic was moving in *any* direction.

I started to ration the bread. The four of us had smoked three more packs of cigarettes, and I opened one of the cans of fruit.

I realized things were getting serious when my wife started sneaking sips of water from *her* liter. Finally we got past the Place, but our hopes that things would ease up along the Quai were shattered when we were stopped again at the Tuileries for two hours.

We had now finished all the cigarettes in the carton and the loaf of bread, and my wife had drunk all her water. Among the five of us, there was only one liter of water left and a can of fruit.

To keep up our courage, we started telling the stories of our lives to each other. Then we started to sing, first "Alouette" and then "God Bless America." But even this paled after a while, and by the time we reached the Louvre we had all become quiet and surly.

Suddenly, the taxi driver, who had remained silent while gnashing his teeth during the trip, became hysterical. He said he saw a green light up ahead and he was going to try to get to it. But it was obviously a mirage, and I gave him some fruit salad to calm him down.

The man who was with us wanted to drink the water in the Seine, but I persuaded him against it.

"Let us all pray," I suggested.

Our prayers must have been answered, because we moved two more blocks.

But we were stuck again by the Châtelet. This time it looked as though we would never move. Then I remembered we were in a radio taxi, and I told the driver to get on the radio and tell his home office what was happening, and to give our position. He tried several times to make contact, but there was no answer.

"Keep trying," I shouted. "Maybe they can hear us and we can't hear them."

Unbeknownst to us, a ham radio operator in Bangor, Maine, picked up our distress signal and relayed it by phone to the French Coast Guard, who sent a helicopter over the Châtelet to find us.

When we heard the whir of the motors, we all jumped out of the taxi and we started waving our shirts. The pilot saw us and hovered over us. First, he picked up the women and flew them over to the Tour d'Argent. Then he picked us up. The taxi driver decided to remain with his cab. As we paid him off, we promised him we'd send help as soon as the cocktail party was over.

By the time we got to the Tour d'Argent, the party was over, but none of us seemed to care. We were alive, and, except for shock, we showed no ill effects from the adventure.

But every once in a while, I wonder what happened to our taxi driver. Like Captain Carlson, he refused to leave his ship. I can only hope for his sake he got another fare.

The Mother Riders

A FOREIGN correspondent has to live with danger. It is his job to go where the story is, no matter what the odds are on his getting back. This is the reason we're all paid $50,000 a year plus expenses. And this is the reason I took on one of the most dangerous assignments in Europe. I rode a school bus from the American School in Paris to the end of the line!

No man other than a bus driver had ever made the trip and lived to tell about it. Only mothers ride the school bus, and they don't do it out of maternal instinct but to protect the bus driver.

It seems that a group of American mothers who lived in the suburbs of Paris discovered there was no bus to take their children to the American School in town. So they banded together and rented a bus, which would pick up the children in the morning and take them home in the afternoon.

The first year they tried it without chaperones, and so many bus drivers quit that the bus company said it wouldn't rent them another bus again unless an adult, other than the bus driver, accompanied the children. The mothers tried to hire paid chaperones but they quit too, so like any group of American mothers, they organized, and decided each day a different mother would ride the bus. They are now known as the Mother Riders of Parents Bus No. 5.

The day I took my ride Mrs. Richard Edelstein, whose husband works for Paramount Pictures, was the Mother of the Day. Mrs. Edelstein has two sons in the American School and she has ridden the bus six times, which is the equivalent of fifty bombing missions in World War II.

The American School has two locations—the lower school is several blocks from the upper school—and our first job was to pick up about twenty children between the ages of six and nine. It was 3:15 and the children piled on the bus and took seats as far away from Mrs. Edelstein as they could possibly get.

The bus started off with a roar and five minutes later we picked up another group of about twenty (you really can't count children on a school bus) between the ages of nine and fourteen.

The bus was fairly quiet when we started because most of the children thought I was a detective that the mothers had hired out of desperation. When they discovered I was nothing but a newspaperman, the wraps were off and they started screaming at each other and swinging their schoolbooks. Mrs. Edelstein had selected a strategic seat in the middle of the bus where she could watch both the back and the front. I crawled under a seat in the back out of the range of fire.

One of the children, Jennifer Cook, explained to me that they had gone through four bus drivers in five months. "The one driving now," she said, "is just a substitute."

"What happened to the last one?" I asked.

"One of the children left a banana peel on the steps of the bus and he slipped and broke his back."

The substitute driver, like all French drivers, raced his bus through the narrow streets of such picturesque towns as St. Cloud, Garches, Vaucresson, La Celle St. Cloud, Bougival, and Malmaison. The only time the driver stopped was to let off a child. Jennifer told me the only other time the driver will stop is when he sees a chum driving another bus. Then both buses stop, windows are rolled down, and the two chums shake hands and chat while the traffic is held up and private cars honk furiously.

Each mother rider has a different approach on Parents Bus No. 5. Mrs. Edelstein, having two young sons, is fairly cool about the whole thing, and will interfere only when actual homicide is being committed. Other mothers are more nervous. One brings candy in hopes of bribing the children into submission.

Another mother, according to two young men who were pulling off each other's coats, takes candy *away* from the children. Mrs. Don Cook, mother of Jennifer, runs a taut ship with no nonsense, while another mother, I was told, sticks cotton in her ears.

The journey took exactly one hour, but for a first-time rider it seemed like the cruise of the Santa Maria. All the children were delivered and we had none left over, though someone named Carl Lovitt left a suitcase full of comic books on board, which were claimed as salvage by the Bougival and Malmaison passengers.

I finally crawled out from my spot under the seat at the last stop in Malmaison, ready to volunteer for the Congo and convinced more than ever that there are no atheists on American School buses in Paris.

5. Et Après, Hong Kong

On to Hong Kong

You get an awful funny reception when you tell someone you're going to Hong Kong.

The first reaction is: "What are you going to do, buy a suit?"

Apparently everyone thinks that you're willing to travel something like 18,000 miles at a cost of $3,000 to buy a suit for $40.00. If you're foolish enough to say you're not going to Hong Kong to buy a suit, then everyone thinks you're going there to meet Suzy Wong.

This didn't go over very big with my wife, who unhappily was not going with me. I have an arrangement whereby I take my wife with me on every *other* trip. I took her to Corsica during the rainy season, I went to Hong Kong alone, but when I got back I took her to visit a new steel mill in the Ruhr Valley. It isn't my fault that the trips fall this way.

As soon as someone hears you're going to Hong Kong alone, he starts leering. One night I had dinner with someone I thought was a friend.

"Boy oh boy," he said, so that my wife was sure to hear him, "there is no town like Hong Kong in the *entire* world. I've been there."

"Yes," I said, "I understand they have a very high cholera rate."

"But," my friend said, "that's not what I'm talking about. They have these dance halls and—"

"They also have a lot of typhoid," I said, trying to shut him up.

"There's a girl in Hong Kong named Annie Ah Har and I'll tell you where you can find her," he said.

"Never mind,' I said, "I only want to talk to refugees from Communist China."

"You ought to talk to Sampan Suzie," "my friend" said. "She'll give you a good story, though you won't be able to print it."

"I won't have time to speak to any of those people," I said. "I understand William Holden is going to be there at that time, and I'll probably spend my evenings with him."

"Not after you meet Sampan Suzie," he said, laughing at his own joke.

The next evening I went out with some other people, but first I made sure they had never been to Hong Kong. It didn't make any difference. When they heard I was going, one of the women said to my wife, "You must be a brave woman to let your husband go to Hong Kong all by himself."

Another woman in the party said to my wife, "I really admire you for being so calm. If *my* husband were going to Hong Kong alone, I would be furious."

"What's wrong with going to Hong Kong alone?" I shouted. "It's the gateway to China. We should know what the enemy is up to. What better listening post is there than Kowloon? If I'm with my wife, no Chinese will talk to me. I owe it to my country to go alone, even incognito, if I have to."

"Newspapermen," said one of the women, "have the most *interesting* jobs."

I must say my wife, in spite of all the innuendoes, was a real sport about letting me go to Hong Kong. She said she trusted me and didn't believe a word anyone said about Hong Kong and Macao and she wanted me to go and believed I should go and she was happy I was going.

Then she gave me a shopping list of all the things she wanted me to buy her in Hong Kong. The list is so long that if I work at it full time it will take me two weeks to get everything on it, which is exactly what she had in mind.

The Mysterious West

IN THE past few years Hong Kong has become the tourist paradise of the Orient. As word has been passed down, from one tourist to another, that you can find Swiss watches in the streets, pick transistor radios off the trees, and receive your weight in Japanese cameras, the pressure on Hong Kong hotels has been so heavy that travel agents have been asked to book their clients a year in advance.

Although in some places tourists are treated as outcasts and with scorn, this is not true of Hong Kong. The Chinese treat them with veneration because they believe that tourists really have the souls of people who are being punished for the wrongs they committed in a former life.

The customs of the tourists are very interesting to study and, while they may seem strange to us, we're sure our customs seem just as strange to them. Tourists have a matriarchal society and women play the dominating role. They lay down the law, and make all the decisions, while the men make the sacrifices.

The most common religious rite performed by the women is called in Chinese Cha-Ping.

To go Cha-Ping is considered by tourist women as the true way to happiness. Some women perform the rite in the morning, while others do it in the afternoon. The most religious women do it all day. The first thing a woman does when she goes Cha-Ping is to put on a cotton robe and low-heeled shoes called flats. Then she takes paper called Mun-Nee and places it in a bag. In order to appease the gods and drive out the evil spirits, the woman must use up the Mun-Nee by sunset.

One of the favorite gods of tourists is the great Bah-Gun. There are great Bah-Guns to be found everywhere in Hong Kong, and every time a woman tourist sees a great Bah-Gun she can't help but stop and burn some Mun-Nee. Women tourists burn Mun-Nee like we Orientals burn incense.

The most sacred days for women tourists are Monday, Tuesday, Wednesday, Thursday, Friday, and Saturday.

On Sunday most of the Bah-Gun temples are closed, though there are Ch'ahps on Nathan Road in Kowloon and Queen's Street in Victoria that stay open for the most faithful.

The men, as I said, play a passive role in tourist society. They wear talismans called Ko-Daks around their necks to ward off the devils, and spend their time waiting for their womenfolk to perform their Chah-Ping. The man tourist is only allowed to take one wife at a time, but if he is unlucky she may turn into a dragon.

To prevent his wife from turning into a dragon, the man tourist believes in getting many good spirits inside him. The most popular tourist spirits are Gin-Fehz, Ska-Che-Aien-Da-Rahd'tks, and Dri-Mah-Tee-Nee. Once the spirits are inside him, the man tourist believes he can stand any pain or disaster. The man tourist believes when he gets enough spirits in him he becomes a tiger. When this happens, the woman tourist sets off fireworks which are supposed to turn the tiger into a lamb.

On the morning after, the man tourist goes through a ritual known as a Hang-Go-Va, which is very painful but good for the soul.

The tourist people also believe in the power of Si-See, in which they sacrifice their feet to appease their conscience. The two most famous Si-See shrines in Hong Kong are Tah-Mahs-Kuk and Ah-Meh-Kan-Ek-Press. These temples provide guides to show you the way. Without them you could get lost. To please Si-See you must wear your feet down to the ankle. Only then may you achieve the true salvation of all tourist people, which is called A-Bah-Tha.

In the evening the tourist people perform a unique ceremony called kicking the gong around. This is a time for feasting and drinking and making new friends.

It is interesting to note that when the tourist people eat food they use strange implements which they call Ni-Fa, Fah-

Cha, and Sup-Na, which are made of metal. For those of us who eat with chopsticks it is difficult to contain ourselves when we see them picking up food with them, and putting it in their mouths.

The tourist people are nomads and do not stay in any place more than a week. When leaving they always take with them a bag of Oh-Va Way-Ta, which they must pay for to the Pan Ah-Meh-Kan bird gods to assure them a safe journey in the sky.

The Best-Dressed Man in Hong Kong

THIS city, which has now become the PX to the world, has a population of 3,239,548 people, of whom 3,239,546 earn their living as tailors.

The making of suits in Hong Kong is the most important industry in the country, and in the struggle for the backs of men, this British crown colony looks like Gimbels basement on a Saturday afternoon before Father's Day.

I didn't realize how important it was to have a suit made in Hong Kong until, after I took off from Rangoon, the stewardess gave me a police card to fill out. It demanded my name, my nationality, my passport number, and wanted to know if I preferred a single- or double-breasted vent in my jacket. I dutifully filled it out and gave it back.

When I landed at the Hong Kong airport I was whisked through the health authorities and sent to customs. The customs inspector asked me: "Do you have anything to declare?" I hesitated for a moment and then decided to come clean. "Yes," I said, "one shoulder is slightly higher than the other." He took his chalk and made a few marks on my sleeve. "Don't worry," he told me, "it will mean an extra fitting, but we'll be able to correct it."

On the airport bus going into town the bus driver, while stopping for a red light, showed me several bolts of cloth. I selected a Dacron-wool mixture which he himself approved of. At the hotel, while I was signing the register, I had my first fitting by the bell captain, who called off the measurements to the room clerk.

Since I had already selected the material on the airport bus, the reception clerk told me there would be no delay in getting my room. On the elevator I had my second fitting, and then while I was waiting for my baggage to be brought up, I had the final fitting.

Before I could get my suitcase open, the completed suit was delivered with sincere apologies for delays and inconveniences caused because the material had to be pre-shrunk before it could be cut.

Since then it's been one fitting after another. I don't really need so many suits, but because I bought one I've been forced to buy the others.

For example, the first evening I was in town I went into a drugstore to buy a toothbrush. While the druggist was wrapping it up he inquired where the new suit I was wearing was made. I said at the hotel, and he shook his head sadly. "They gave you a split sleeve with a slanted cuff and flap pockets."

"Is there anything I can do about it?" I asked nervously.

"Well, I'm not a doctor," he said, "but I'll see what I can do."

He took a bolt of English herringbone cloth out of one of the medicine cabinets and let me look at the magazines while he cut the pattern. In half an hour the suit was ready, and he was so proud of his work he told me: "You look so nice in my suit you can now meet a beautiful dance girl at Princess Garden."

He gave me the address and I rushed over. The Princess Garden is a famous Hong Kong restaurant and dance hall. You pay a dollar and forty cents an hour to dance with a beautiful Chinese girl or ten dollars for four hours, whichever is more.

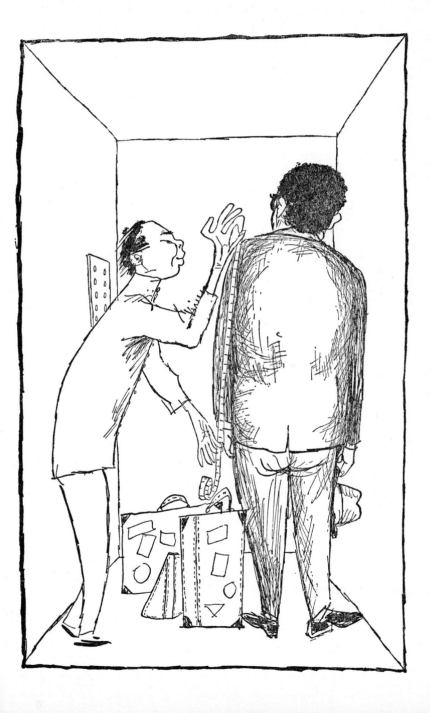

It must have been my new suit, because as soon as I was seated a woman who looked like a combination of Suzie Wong and the Dragon Lady came over to the table and sat down.

"You beautiful American man," she said, taking my hand in hers. "We dance for little while and then go to my place."

"Well, really," I said feverishly.

"Don't worry," she said, "I make you very happy."

An hour later we arrived at her apartment. She opened the door and took my hand and led me in. Then she turned on the lights. Seated in every corner of the room was a member of her family at a sewing machine. Her father started taking the measurements and damned if I didn't wind up with another suit.

Scrubbing Bill Holden's Back

I HAD dinner one night with Mr. and Mrs. William Holden. Mr. Holden was in Hong Kong remaking *The World of Suzie Wong.* Mr. Holden made most of it once with France Nuyen but, due to circumstances, he had to do it over again with a new Suzie Wong named Nancy Kwan.

Mr. Holden said he didn't mind making the same picture twice. For one thing, he believed it would be a better picture with Miss Kwan, and for another he liked Hong Kong. He liked it so much he bought into a Hong Kong commercial radio station a few years ago, and he said he plans to spend about three months a year out here commuting between Hong Kong and Tokyo. (In Tokyo he owns a piece of the Ho-Sho Electronics Company which makes computers and transistors.)

"I have a rooting interest in these companies," he said, "but even if I didn't I'd still come to the Far East."

One of the things that came out of the dinner was that Mr. Holden liked the deference an Oriental woman paid a male. Mrs. Holden wasn't too sure if she liked it or not.

"The Oriental woman," said Mr. Holden, "has a charm and a dignity a Western woman lacks."

"My foot," said Mrs. Holden. "If I giggled the way Oriental women do you'd throw me out of the house. I agree they have a certain charm and dignity, but the very things you admire in an Oriental woman you wouldn't stand for in an American woman."

Mr. Holden held up his hand, but Mrs. Holden continued:

"Your attitude toward an Oriental woman is the same as toward a child. But you want your Western woman to be on the beam. We're supposed to read books and newspapers and be able to discuss baseball. All you want an Oriental woman to do is scrub your back in the bathtub."

I turned to Mr. Holden.

"What do you have to say to that, sir?"

"Phooey," he said, "and you may quote me."

"Don't say 'phooey,'" Mrs. Holden said. "When you're in the bathtub and I ask if you want your back scrubbed, you say get off it."

"Well," said Mr. Holden, "I know you don't mean it. It's just a gesture of courtesy. When a Western woman offers to scrub your back it's just pap talk that goes on in the Western world, like 'Did you have a good day at the office?' When an Oriental woman offers to scrub your back she means it."

"I mean it too," Mrs. Holden almost shouted.

I looked at Mr. Holden. He seemed to be phrasing his words very carefully.

"The difference between an Oriental woman and a Western woman is that an Oriental woman scrubs your back without asking."

The three of us ate in silence. Finally Mrs. Holden said:

"Listen. I'm partial to Eastern women, but if I tried to mold myself along those lines I'd immediately be suspected of being up to no good. It's like the Chinese dresses with the slits along the sides. They look beautiful on a Chinese woman, but a Western woman could never wear them."

"That is a point," I said to Mr. Holden. Mr. Holden didn't seem to be listening.

"One of the nice things about Oriental women is that at the end of the day they never tell you what they've done for you. Western women can't wait to tell what they've done for their husbands."

"He's right there," I said to Mrs. Holden.

"What do you want us to be?" Mrs. Holden asked. "A bunch of stupid listeners? If we were quiet for more than two hours you'd call for the doctor."

"I may be old-fashioned," Mr. Holden said, "but I believe that dogs, walnut trees, and women are only good if you beat them, and the more you beat them the better they get."

"I must agree with him, as much as I don't want to," I said to Mrs. Holden.

Once again there was dead silence. To get things back on an even keel, I said to Mr. Holden:

"How can a Western woman, without any Oriental background, make her husband happy?"

"Well, for a starter," he said, "she can scrub his back without asking him."

It seemed to me to be a gesture in the right direction.

Our Man in Hong Kong, or the Honest American

I WAS sitting in the Sun Ya restaurant in Hong Kong nibbling on a bear claw, back in May 1960, just after the U-2 incident, when a man in a tweed suit, smoking a pipe, sat down at the next table. He ordered a bowl of bird's-nest soup, and when it arrived he started to develop a role of microfilm in it.

When he saw me staring at him he said, very quietly, "Beeswhipple, British Intelligence."

I stuck out my hand. "Buchwald, Lockheed Aircraft."

"I knew you were one of us the minute I sat down," he said confidentially.

"How could you possibly have known?"

He smiled. "Your oxygen mask is sticking out of your undershirt."

I looked down and hastily shoved the mask back in.

"I see where one of your chaps got his hand caught in the cooky jar the other day," he said.

"Yup," I said. "But it could have happened to anybody."

He ordered a bowl of braised fish lips.

"I daresay not. It could have never happened to us."

"Why not?" I asked, sticking a chopstick into a shark's fin.

"We have a different attitude toward such things. You Americans don't seem to understand too much about this business. If one of our chaps had been caught, we would have played it entirely differently."

"How's that?"

"Well, the first thing we would have done is announce that somebody stole one of our weather planes from a Turkish airport and Her Majesty's Government was offering a hundred guineas' reward for the return of the plane and the pilot."

"But that would be lying," I said, trying to keep the shock out of my voice.

"Precisely, my dear fellow."

"But we're not allowed to lie in the American intelligence system. It encourages bad character. The State Department would never stand for it. Our slogan is: "We tell the truth and let the planes fall where they may."

Beeswhipple poured some jasmine tea on the tablecloth and the linen suddenly turned into a map showing every military airfield in southwest China. He pocketed the tablecloth and popped a tuna-fish eyeball into his mouth.

"We're not saying you should lie," he said. "We're not saying you should say anything. But, after all, you could show a little indignation when someone steals one of your aircraft."

"But he didn't steal it," I said. "He was told to fly over Russia and take pictures. We've been doing it for four years. Frankly, we were afraid no one would *ever* hear about it. Now the air is cleared. All of this was part of Eisenhower's Open Spies Policy."

Beeswhipple picked up a fortune cookie and when he broke it open he took out the order of battle for the North Korean Army.

I couldn't help feeling a pang of jealousy.

"My dear fellow," Beeswhipple said, "no one admires candor more than the British, but we treat the stealing of unmarked airplanes as a very serious offense, and we certainly take a dim view of someone making his escape over the Soviet Union."

"You just don't seem to understand," I protested. "Lying in spying is the coward's way out. If we tell lies, then the Russians will tell lies. You've got to call a spy a spy.

"This is only the beginning. It's our hope that in the not too distant future we'll have spy exchange fellowships, and the Russians will send us their spies and we'll send them ours, on a Fulbright scholarship. Until this exchange can be worked out we'll just have to keep flying over their territory."

Beeswhipple unscrewed the top of the soy sauce bottle and pried out a blueprint of the latest Russian spaceship.

"I can hardly agree with you," he said. "If the chap was really working for the CIA, as the Russians ridiculously claim, how do they explain the wedding rings they found on him? It's obvious he was mixed up in a white-slavery racket, and this was not a case for the State Department but for Interpol."

I was becoming angry. "There is no sense talking to you. You just weren't brought up in the American tradition of fair play. When we get caught doing something we believe in making a clean breast of it. Charles Van Doren has shown us the way."

I gave the waiter my CIA Diner's Club Credit Card,

signed the check, and left Beeswhipple trying to get a model
of an atomic submarine out of a sweet-and-sour lobster.
What he didn't know about espionage could fill a book.

Fortunetelling on Cat Street

ONE of the first things you should do when you come to
Hong Kong is have your fortune told. It is said that eight
out of ten Chinese in Hong Kong believe in fortunetelling and
the other two are fortunetellers. No one makes a move here
without first consulting the signs. Even going to the barber
is something that shouldn't be left to chance.

For example, if you get a shampoo on the First of the
Moon you're only shortening your life expectancy. The second and third days are lucky to get a haircut, but if you
do it on the fifth day your hair is going to fall out. A haircut on the twelfth means trouble, but if you get one on the
thirteenth you're going to have a gift of sons.

It's this kind of information a tourist should be aware of,
and so I hied myself off to Cat Street, the Flea Market of
Hong Kong, where some of the great fortunetellers of the
city hold court. I took an interpreter along. There is no
sense in having your fortune told if you don't know what
the fortuneteller is telling you.

Through the interpreter, I was told the fortunetelling
would cost me the equivalent of five American dollars. This
is rather high for Hong Kong and I objected. But the fortuneteller said: "Here we only tell the truth. If we say it
costs five dollars to tell your fortune, that's the truth."

Chinese fortunetellers use many methods of looking into
the future; the most popular is the study of the palms and
face. Chicken, snake, or rat eyes, it is said, show you have
a great fondness for the opposite sex, while large round eyes

with a shifty glance indicate a cruel nature. (This is a Chinese interpretation, mind you; Caucasian fortunetellers will tell you exactly the opposite.)

The Chinese divide the face into three parts: the forehead, representing heaven; the chin, earth; and the nose, human inhabitants. If you want a long life your chin should be wide and square. The rounder your forehead the better chance you have for early distinction and a happy childhood, and the larger your nostrils the richer you'll be.

The fortuneteller studied my face for a few moments and then said: "You've come a long way."

I could tell he knew his stuff.

He felt the bumps on my head. "You are not going to make any progress financially for the next year." This was true, but how he knew it I'll never know.

"But if you do good deeds, nothing bad will happen to you. In the next few weeks you will spend more money than you make." The fortuneteller was absolutely clairvoyant.

"Your money is in wood, but metal is overtaking wood." Should I sell International Paper and buy U. S. Steel?

He told me that I might have some reverses in the next few weeks, "but although I'd scar the table, the table itself was too strong to be destroyed."

At the time my fortune was being told a thousand U. S. marines off the carrier *Princeton* were in town and I suspect he thought I came from there, because he said, after touching my eyebrows, "You are going to be a general."

He advised me to keep cleanly shaved and never to grow a mustache. Apparently I was under the sign of the Black Dragon and a mustache would only distract the dragon from the rest of my face.

"You shouldn't marry too early." It was uncanny. Once again he hit right on the nose. "I am married," I said.

He touched my left ear. "Then you have a good wife."

"People are jealous of your power," he said. He couldn't possibly know about Jim Hagerty.

"You shouldn't drink too much or you will get into arguments." Maybe he *did* know about Jim Hagerty.

He took one more reading on my cheekbones and then he told me: "The next two weeks you will travel and meet many people. Southwest is your favorable direction. Do not go north."

"I shouldn't go to Communist China?"

"That's right," the fortuneteller said.

I rose in a huff. "The American Embassy tells you the same thing, and they don't charge five dollars."

Mary Soo, Queen of the Garbage

THE United States Seventh Fleet, which plies its trade in the troubled waters of the Far East, has a girl friend named Mary Soo. Mary Soo, by tradition but not contract, has the garbage concession of all United States Navy ships entering Hong Kong, which out here is no small potatoes.

In exchange for the garbage, Mary Soo provides crews of Chinese women to paint the sides of Navy ships while they are in port. The Navy supplies the paint and Mary Soo does the work for free.

It's a happy arrangement for everybody. The Navy gets rid of its garbage, the American sailors who might have to spend their time chipping and painting the sides of the ships are free to go on liberty into Hong Kong, and Mary Soo, who has a market for refuse, is said to be the richest garbage collector in the colony.

Garbage-collecting in Hong Kong Harbor is a very tough business and a competitor would just as soon slit your sampan as look at you. Despite the competition, Mary Soo, with the exception of the war years, has had the exclusive rights to American leftovers for twenty-seven years.

It is an unwritten rule of the Seventh Fleet that only Mary Soo's girls may come aboard a United States Navy ship in Hong Kong.

Hong Kong is considered a recreation port for the fleet, and

during a tour every ship in the fleet usually drops in for a six-day period. Mary Soo has a flag for every ship in the American Navy and usually the first one to greet a new arrival is Mary Soo on her sampan, flying the name of the ship from her mast. It is said that Mary Soo knows more through the grapevine about the movements of the fleet than the Pentagon.

As soon as a ship drops anchor, Mary Soo goes aboard with her girls, who start hauling off the garbage into the sampans. Mary Soo pays a courtesy call on the executive officers to be polite, but as soon as this is over she immediately heads for the chief petty officers' wardroom, where she is greeted by the chiefs, some of whom have known her for twenty years. Mary Soo's love affair with the Seventh Fleet is not with the officers but with the enlisted men. As long as the ship is in port she makes her headquarters in the chiefs' quarters, where she is treated like a queen.

It was in the chief petty officers' wardroom on the U. S. S. *Arnold J. Isobell*, a destroyer, that I found her drinking coffee one afternoon. It seems Mary Soo has two main interests, garbage and leftovers. Garbage is collected to be sold to farmers for their livestock, and the leftovers are sold to Chinese refugees.

"Good chow for eat," Mary Soo said. "No good chow give piggy."

"Don't let her kid you," one of the chiefs said, "she sells the leftovers to the best restaurant in Hong Kong."

"He makey joke joke," Mary Soo said.

In order to insure that the leftovers and the garbage don't get mixed, Mary Soo stations one of her girls in each of the ship's messes and the sailors turn over their trays to her when they've finished eating. This is the good chow "for eat." Also any chow still left in the serving pans after the meal is over belongs to Mary Soo.

Some days are better than others on the *Isobell*. For example, Wednesday is Chicken Day and Sunday is Steak Day, and the leftovers on these days are much in demand.

While Mary Soo is down in the chiefs' quarters, her crew of women, working with long bamboo poles on sampans, are painting the sides of the ship. She said it takes a day to paint a destroyer hull, two days to paint a cruiser, and four days to paint an aircraft carrier.

Mary Soo prefers using women to men because men "no good work work. Girls good work work if not too old or too young. Best girls between nineteen and twenty-five." Mary Soo looks after her girls like a sorority mother and allows no fraternization with the sailors. One of the chiefs said: "Don't let her kid you. All her girls are really yum yum girls from the dance halls."

Mary Soo slammed down her cup of coffee and scowled. "You fat liar. My girls no yum yum girls. They good work work girls."

Mary Soo explained that she is so famous that many dance hall girls claim they work for her just to win favor with the American sailors.

Besides garbage, Mary Soo also collects old rope, old mattresses, junk, and dunnage, which she keeps in a warehouse. When the sailors know they're coming to Hong Kong, they put aside for her everything they would ordinarily throw away.

In exchange Mary Soo paints the hull, reads the palms of sailors, gives them artificial flowers for their mess halls, and when a favorite ship is ready to leave Hong Kong she puts on a firework display on her sampan to wish the crew bon voyage. The highest tribute a sailor can pay Mary Soo is to lose his appetite on board ship in Hong Kong.

Hit Him Below the Belt!

FRIENDS of mine can't understand why I wasn't more excited about the Floyd Patterson-Ingemar Johansson fight.

The reason is that I recently spent a few days in Bangkok, Thailand, and after seeing Thai boxing I'll never be happy with Western-style boxing again.

Thai boxing differs from our boxing in that the fighters are permitted, even encouraged, to use, besides their fists, their elbows, knees, and feet. There is no rule against hitting below the belt and practically anything but biting is permitted.

This leads to some very interesting contests.

Boxing is to the Thai what bullfighting is to the Spaniard. Matches are held in Bangkok four times a week, at five o'clock in the afternoon. Unlike bullfighting, though, one of the main features of Thai boxing is gambling on the outcome.

When I entered the arena at Rajadamnon Stadium, a three-piece band, consisting of a pipe and two long drums, was playing ferociously. Thai boxing fans can be excitable, and a barbed-wire fence separated the grandstand fans from the ringside seats.

There were seven bouts of five rounds each. I was given a program in English which gave a rundown on the fighters.

The flashing star of Udorndhanee, who was named Krais-horn-Thaung, was described as follows: "Experienced in style advancing lead followed by kick to land in the solar plexus or on chin, and sends opponents to dreamland."

Manusak, his worthy opponent, was "a lion-hearted typhoon who loves to march forward without retreating, if received hurt or cut."

Before the fight started, both opponents came in to the center of the ring, knelt, and prayed. This was followed by a Thai dance in which each fighter described in ballet form what he would do to his opponent. The band provided the music for the dance. All fights, I was told, start with a prayer and then a "strike fear into the hearts of their opponents" dance.

In the first round Manusak struck a blow to the kidneys with his left foot. Kraishorn-Thaung retaliated with an elbow in Manusak's neck. Manusak smashed a knee to the groin, but Kraishorn-Thaung recovered and let fly his foot to Manusak's jaw.

It was a close fight, but Manusak won by a decision.

The next fight was between Krai-Raj, who, according to the program, "worships the 'do or die' motto, once in the ring it is either his opponent is carried down or he is carried out to the hospital. He is known as a kicking knockout artist among fans in the mitt circle."

Krai-Raj's opponent, Khuntaal, was a "famous speed merchant lion-hearted, used to absorbing great punishment and is known to hang a dangerous kick on opponents' chins and let them dream happily."

Khuntaal flailed away with his feet and instead of being sent to the hospital his ankle blows to Krai-Raj's head forced Krai-Raj to give up while still standing on his feet, though not knowing where he was.

The main event found in one corner Visnusingh, "the best product of the cauliflower industry of Saraburi—a lickety-split kid devastating and damaging, who always gives the referees some jobs to do in singing one-two-ten into opponent's ears, whilst he is dreaming happily."

In the other corner was Chatramanee, no pushover, according to my program.

He was "a valuable product of the mitt industry of Korat—a tough aggressive wildcat whose assets of fighting are speedy terrific hitting and dangerous highkick which provide sensation for fans to be long remembered."

Visnusingh was confident, perhaps overly so. He tried to smash Chatramanee in the face with his knees, but the Korat Wildcat swung the Lickety-Split Kid around and let him have several elbows in the solar plexus.

Visnusingh in the second round managed to land a shin on Chatramanee's neck, but only stunned him for a moment. Chatramanee came back and put his foot into Visnusingh's face, causing Visnusingh great pain and embarrassment. In the third round Visnusingh, on instructions from his manager, let a limb fly at Chatramanee's jaw and followed it by pounding his buttocks in a clinch. Chatramanee disengaged himself and landed with his famous high kick to the Lickety-Split Kid's jaw, thus knocking out the pride of the cauliflower industry and making the referee sing into his ear one-two-ten whilst he dreamed.

It was a great fight, Mom, and now you can see why the Patterson-Johansson fight didn't mean much to me. Those kids in the U. S. were just tea-dancing.

Not Covered by Blue Cross

MANY people have been kind enough to write me as to the status of the suits I bought in Hong Kong. I bought three suits at the going rate of twenty-five dollars each, and all were delivered within twenty-four hours with my name personally sewn in the inside coat pocket.

I'm happy to report that all three suits have held up remarkably well. The fawn-colored lightweight easy-to-wash seersucker was laundered the other day and although one pant leg shrank six inches, my name in the inside pocket did not shrink at all.

The hair-striped sharkskin lounge suit, which my Hong Kong tailor told me was the latest thing Jack Paar was wearing, has also held up remarkably well, except for the pants pockets, which keep slipping down, forcing my keys to fall out.

The only suit I've really had any trouble with has been a gray flannel two-button daytime model which, according to the Chinese tailor, could be handed down from father to son for the next five generations. The suit never did feel exactly right, even when I tried it on in Hong Kong, but the tailor assured me that this was because of the Kowloon humidity, and once I went to a dryer climate it would fit like a glove.

If I had thought it out at the time, I really didn't want the suit to fit like a glove—I wanted it to fit like a suit.

Since I had to make a short trip to London, I decided to bring the suit over and take it to a Savile Row tailor and see if he could do anything with it.

Rather than drag it with me, I chose to wear it over to the tailor's.

When I walked in, one of the tailors rushed over and said: "What happened, sir? Were you in an accident?" "No," I explained, "I bought this suit in Hong Kong and it doesn't seem to fit quite right. I was wondering . . ."

The tailor stared at the costume. "Then, that is your surr?"

I nodded. He shook his head. "I'm afraid, sir, the kindest thing we could do is take it out in the back yard and shoot it."

"No," I cried, "I paid twenty-five dollars for this suit, and I'm sure with just a few minor alterations it could be made wearable."

The tailor was reluctant to touch it. "I'll have to call in a specialist," he said. "I don't want to take the responsibility for this."

He called over another tailor, who turned white when he saw the suit.

He muttered: "It's the worst case of Hong Kong suiting I've ever seen. There are multiple fractures of the center vent, bad cuts over the slant pockets, abrasions on the seat seam, high waist suppression, and the shoulders have to be completely relined. We'll have to operate at once."

"You're the doctor," I said nervously.

"Even if we can save the right pants leg, which I doubt," he warned, "you'll never have more than 50 per cent use of your cuffs again."

"It's better than having them cut off," I said, trying to cheer him up.

"Your left sleeve will have to be put in traction for three months."

"It could be worse," I replied, trying to keep a stiff upper lip.

"And I'll have to put a cast on the collar until it can mend."

"Will it be painful?" I wanted to know.

"These things are never easy. You see, although we've made great strides in tailoring, we still haven't discovered a cure for a Hong Kong suit. Perhaps someone will invent a miracle fabric some day, but until then we must rely on plastic surgery."

They took me into the operating room. While two tailors held me down, the third started to work on me with a needle and scissors.

No matter how brave I tried to be, my screams could be heard as far away as Oxford Street.

But three hours later I limped out, practically a new man. Saving a Hong Kong suit does not come under Blue Cross and I had to pay for the operation in cash. It cost me ninety dollars, but it was worth it. Unless you looked at the label you would never know where the suit came from. And the only time it hurts is when it rains.

6. En Voyage

The Smashing Tailors of Beersheba

THERE has been a great deal of excitement in the United States and Israel over suspicions that Israel might be working on the development of an atomic bomb.

Apparently United States State Department officials are furious because, when the Israelis built their atomic energy plant twenty miles outside of Beersheba, they told the United States it was a textile plant. The United States was kept in the dark until recently, when CIA photographs revealed that the building wasn't what it was cracked up to be.

It was just by chance that the Americans didn't find out the secret six months ago.

I heard the following story from an Israeli taxi driver high in government circles.

It seems that an important American diplomat stationed in Israel needed a new suit, and since someone told him about the new textile plant he decided to go out there and see if he could possibly get one wholesale.

As he drove south toward Beersheba, Israeli intelligence agents were alerted and a half-hour before he got there the head of the atomic energy plant was notified that an American was coming to buy a suit.

A hurried conference was called with the other scientists to decide what to do. They were afraid that if they refused him entrance he might get suspicious and start prying into the plant, so the scientists agreed the only sensible thing to do was let the diplomat in and pretend that nothing was going on.

The scientists all removed their white smocks, rolled up their sleeves, and stuck pins and needles in their vests.

When the American diplomat arrived, he was immediately

ushered into a large room where he saw men cutting suit forms out of asbestos patterns.

The head of the plant greeted the diplomat. "What can I do for you, sir?" he asked.

"I was wondering if I could buy a suit wholesale?"

"Naturally. That is what we make here. What did you have in mind?"

"Well, what do you have?"

The head of the plant said: "Perhaps you would like something in cobalt blue? Or maybe a nice uranium brown? How about a cosmic gray double-breasted, with pin-striped particles. It's the latest thing."

"No," said the diplomat, "I don't want anything flashy. You wouldn't have a light gray flannel?"

"Perhaps," the head said. "Please, let us take your measurements. Just go in the fitting room behind that six-foot wall of lead and take off your clothes."

The diplomat went in. "These fitting rooms are very well protected," he said.

The head of the plant smiled. "Our customers like privacy and there's so much activity around here that we don't like things to pile up. Just a minute, I'll call the fitter. Shimshon, would you please come in with the measuring instruments."

One of the scientists rushed in with a Geiger counter, a slide rule, and two robot arms. The head of the plant took a pad and said: "Shimshon, call off the customer's measurements."

Shimshon yelled out: "Ten, nine, eight, seven, six, five, four, three, two, one, oi!"

"What kind of measurements are those?" the diplomat wanted to know.

"Enough with the jokes, Shimshon," the head said angrily, "let's have the measurements."

Shimshon chuckled and called out: "Waist U-235; relativity good chest; there is a hexagonal prism in the left shoulder; the right sleeve needs reactor."

"What about the lapels?" the diplomat wanted to know.

"Don't worry," Shimshon said, "we'll smash them down if they're too large."

Shimshon measured the pants and then the diplomat put on his clothes again. "Don't you have any materials to show me?" the diplomat asked.

"Are you interested in camel's hair?" the head of the plant wanted to know.

"I might be," the diplomat said. "Do you have any swatches?"

The head of the plant said: "We'll do better than that. Kishon, the man is interested in a camel's-hair suit."

One of the other scientists ran out of the shop and five minutes later brought in a camel which he had borrowed from an Arab nomad.

The head of the plant said proudly: "Here we don't fool around with swatches. Here the customer sees the entire camel."

"All right," the diplomat said. "Can I charge it?"

"Negative or positive?" the head of the plant wanted to know.

"I don't care," the diplomat said. "When should I come for my next fitting?"

The head of the plant said: "Why should you, an important man, drive to Beersheba again? Our tailor from our retail store in Tel Aviv will call on you. You of course will be entitled to our wholesale price. But please, kind sir, *do not* tell your friends about us because we have too much work now, and if we take any more orders the plant will explode."

The Matchmaker

ONE of the most interesting of all professions in Israel is that of the marriage broker, or, as it is known here, the shadkhan.

The Jewish marriage broker, famed in song and story, has

through the ages served the role of finding the right Jewish girl for the right Jewish man and has acted as the negotiator in the tricky business of dowries that every father must pay if he wants to get his daughter out of the house. Although more and more Israelis prefer to find their own spouses, there is still a thriving marriage-broker business in Israel. I had the pleasure of visiting one of the better-known matchmakers, a Mrs. Eliza of Tel Aviv, who has been bringing people together for the past fifteen years.

Mrs. Eliza, who learned the business from her father, is one of the most imaginative of all marriage brokers and can be credited with holding the first international festival of unmarried people in Tel Aviv, in which 230 people, many sent by matchmakers abroad, participated. It was a great success and quite a few marriages came out of it. Professional matchmaking is a job not to be treated lightly, Mrs. Eliza told me. There are many things to be taken into consideration before you find the right partners, and while the profession is not a licensed one, there are many ethics involved.

For example, if a man just wants to marry a girl for money, Mrs. Eliza refuses to take the client. "I want my people to marry for love," she told me. "I want that my clients should be healthy in spirit and body."

The average dowry now being offered on the Israeli marriage market is £5,000 or $2,500, though Mrs. Eliza showed me pictures of some girls whose fathers were willing to pay £25,000 for a husband.

She has had clients from every walk of life: soldiers, divorcees, Yemenite women—much sought after by Austrian and German men—girls on co-operative farms, and men and women of every nationality.

Mrs. Eliza operates as follows: a person comes in and registers with her. The matchmaker writes down what he or she has in mind. The client puts down a deposit and then promises that if he meets a mate through Mrs. Eliza he'll pay her a fee which could be anywhere from seventy-five to

two hundred dollars, depending on how much dowry is
involved. Then Mrs. Eliza starts matching.

She has many ways of introducing the clients. One of the
most popular is for the man to buy two reserved seats in a
cinema. One is given to the girl and he keeps the other. Then
they meet in the movie.

They look at each other in the dark and then the man
decides whether he wants to continue with the romance,
usually by inviting the girl out for coffee at a café. If not,
he watches the movie and goes home alone.

Mrs. Eliza says she's very strict about her clients: "If a
girl reports to me a client kissed her without permission I
refuse to handle him from then on. I tell all my women clients
not to do much kissing. The less they do the more the men
will want to marry them."

The toughest part of the marriage-broker business, Mrs.
Eliza said, is trying to collect from the clients after they get
married. "Nobody likes to pay the matchmaker," she complained, "and they always minimize my role in the match
in hopes of getting the fee down.

"One man refused to pay me, so I sent my husband to
see him. 'I don't have the money,' the man said, 'so you
can have my wife back.'"

As to dowries, occasionally a girl may exaggerate the size
of the dowry. What happens in this case? Mrs. Eliza said that
if the husband finds he has married a nice girl he doesn't
make a point of it, but if he finds she's a disappointment he
asks where the money is.

The matchmaker said she married one of her own clients
ten years ago. "A man came in and said he wanted to find
a wife but when he tried to explain the kind of woman he
wanted all he could say was, 'I want somebody like you,'
so two weeks later we were married."

Of all the incidents in her career, the most dramatic concerned a young girl crippled with polio who came to Mrs.
Eliza in hopes of finding a husband.

"I knew I could do nothing for her," Mrs. Eliza said, "but

didn't have the heart to tell her, so I went through the motions of interviewing her and told her to come back in a week.

"She came back and while she was waiting in the foyer I interviewed a very nice young Czechoslovakian boy. I said to him, 'I will find you a very pretty girl but first I have a favor to ask of you. Would you take the girl sitting out in the foyer to a café and pretend you might be interested in her? I will pay you for whatever it costs but you would make her happy.'

"The boy said I didn't have to pay him anything, he would do it as a courtesy. Well, I'm sure you know the end of the story. He fell in love with her and now they are happily married and it's the nicest match I ever made."

Anyone for Golf?

THE last time I was in Israel was many years ago, and I must admit there have been quite a few changes. The first thing people asked me in those days was: "Have you seen our Huleh project?" The Huleh project was a valley which the Israelis had drained, thus adding thousands of acres of arable land, and the Israelis were quite proud of it.

But times have changed even in Israel, and this time the first question almost everyone has asked me is: "Have you seen our new golf course?" Israel hasn't had a golf course for two thousand years (there is a theory the Romans used to play a similar game, but with IX instead of XVIII holes), and they are bursting with pride in spite of the fact not too many people here know exactly what golf is.

They say that three years ago an American newspaperman got up at a press conference given by Premier David Ben-Gurion and said: "Mr. Prime Minister, is it true you are building a golf course so you can invite President Eisenhower to Israel?"

The Prime Minister looked startled and whispered to his aid: "What is golf?"

"It's a game," the aid whispered back.

The Prime Minister said to the American newspaperman: "No, I don't play games."

Israel's first golf course is located at Caesarea, ancient port of the Roman legions. The land and the course belong to the Rothschild family and it's a private club with about 250 members.

The course is bordered on one side by the sea and on the other side by Jordan. If you slice the ball, you go in the ocean. If you hook it, you can start a war. If you hit an Arab, the United Nations penalizes you two strokes.

The other problem of Caesarea is the sand traps. Since Caesarea has so many ruins, somebody who finds himself in a sand trap might dig up an entire Phoenician city with his niblick, in which case he's not allowed to blast out until a member of the Israeli archaeological society arrives. Something like this can hold up a game for days.

In discussing golf with our Israeli friends, I discovered they had varied opinions on it. One said: "We only had room for nine holes, and since we wanted eighteen we had to launch the Sinai campaign. The Gaza Strip would have made a wonderful parking lot."

There are no books in Hebrew on golf, and some of the members still haven't got the hang of the game. I met one member who never played, and another who had been a member for ten months and went seven holes before he gave up. A lady member, Miss Sharona Aron, an Israeli singer of fame, told me she was taking lessons.

"What's par for the course?" I asked.

Miss Aron shrugged her shoulders: "Who knows?"

The favorite day for golf in Israel is Saturday, the day of rest, just as the favorite day in the Christian world is Sunday. This has caused a certain amount of consternation in religious circles down here, but the Israeli golf players answer the criticism like true golfers anywhere: "When else can we play?"

Brides Over Berlin

THE United States Army wives of West Berlin are holding classes for German brides of American GIs to help them become good American wives.

The courses are held once a week and I was happy to attend one in the apartment of Mrs. R. G. Ament, an officer's wife, who with a Mrs. Vern Pike, and a Mrs. D. C. Green, also officers' wives, were instructing five German wives and two fiancées in the delicate art of being an American wife.

It's very difficult to know what to call the German-born wife of an American soldier. When I referred to them as "war brides" they bridled. When I suggested they were "cold war brides" they were horrified, and when I asked if I could call them "peace brides" they all said no.

When I arrived the class was in session and Mrs. Green was reading from a book called *The Army Wife* on how to give a formal tea, which included instructions on polishing silver, making a cake, serving the tea, and wearing a hat.

As a graduation exercise the brides were going to give a tea, and one of the reasons Mrs. Ament, Mrs. Pike, and Mrs. Green were reading from the book was that none of them had ever given a tea, and the teachers were as perplexed about it as the pupils.

So far the brides have learned how to prepare an American breakfast, and how to make grilled cheese, tuna fish, and bacon and tomato and lettuce sandwiches for lunch. They have also seen films on the United States. One film called *Smalltown, U.S.A.* made every one of the brides decide they wanted to live in a big city.

All the brides said they enjoyed the way American men treated them, as opposed to German men. "Ve haf more freedom as American vifes," one of the ladies said.

On the other hand, one of the brides said her husband didn't want her to become an American wife. "He said he married a European wife. If he wanted an American for a wife he would have married one."

I asked the brides what they would do if they were teaching an American girl how to be a good German wife.

One young lady said: "I pity any girl who marries a German. When you marry a German man you have to be a slave."

Another one said: "German husbands don't want their wives to be seen outside when they're pregnant. They're ashamed of them."

A third one added: "You must never ask a German husband to do anything in the house. He doesn't want to know anything about the kitchen. All he wants is his slippers and his newspaper."

A fourth young lady said: "He doesn't really read the newspaper. He just looks out from behind to see what you're doing wrong."

"I would tell an American girl if she married a German," another bride said, "not to say anything at the dinner table. A German husband doesn't want conversation with his meals."

"What would you serve a German husband for breakfast?" I asked.

"Cheese, sausage, rolls, and sometimes soup."

"And dinner?"

"Anything, as long as it has lots of potatoes."

One of the German brides said German husbands make their wives wait a long time for children. "First they want a TV set, then an icebox, then a car. After they get the stuff, then they will agree to have a baby."

They all agreed they had much more chance of becoming "the boss" with an American husband than a German one.

The entire meeting sounded subversive to me and the American Army wives seemed to be destroying all the slave-like qualities that the American husbands had once seen in their German wives. But I was outnumbered, so I kept my mouth shut—that is, until Mrs. Green, in describing the American way of life, said to the girls: "And remember, never wear rhinestones before six o'clock."

That was too much, even for me.

East German Betting

ONE of the last bastions of free enterprise in the otherwise Communized city of East Berlin is the East German horse parlor, or what we jaded capitalists like to refer to as a bookie joint. Much to everyone's surprise, there exist in East Berlin at this moment thirteen horse parlors, privately owned by East German bookies, with the blessing of the Communist state, which takes its bite out of the oppressed bettors' winnings.

It is not the fact that East Germany allows its citizens to bet on the ponies that surprised me but what ponies they allow them to bet on. The East Germans bet on races running in the decadent city of Paris, at such imperialist tracks as Longchamp, St. Cloud, Auteuil, and Vincennes, and despite the fact that there hasn't been any telephone communication between East Berlin and West Berlin since May 1952, the results of all French races are telephoned from West Berlin to East Berlin within three minutes of their running.

Also the only West German newspaper sold in East Berlin is the *Jockey,* a racing form sheet which is published in Cologne. Without the form sheet it would be impossible for the East Berlin horse players to bet on the French races, because many of them have not only never seen a horse race they have never seen a horse.

I stopped in the horse parlor in East Berlin next to the Hotel Niva in the middle of the afternoon. It looked like any horse parlor anywhere. About thirty men were busy studying their forms with poised pencils, a few were making bets, and one or two were walking around touting their friends. My arrival caused little stir, as horse players are used to any kind of characters in a horse parlor, and if someone wanted to look and dress like an American, the horse players figured it was none of their business.

It was only after I got to talking to a few of them—one man spoke English, another French—that they became interested in the fact I lived in Paris and had actually seen those faraway mysterious places and the animals that had been taking so much of their time and all their money.

I tried to describe each track for them in detail, putting as much feeling into it as I could. Tears came to their eyes as I talked of the infield at Longchamp and the paddock at Chantilly. To them St. Cloud was Mecca and you could feel that they believed if they could just get to the French tracks and see the horses for themselves their selecting problems would be solved.

Almost every East Berlin horse player, I was led to believe, has a plan. First, he hopes to win enough money playing the horses in an East German horse parlor so he can go over to a West Berlin horse parlor and play the same horses there which, because of money difficulties, is four times as expensive. Then, if he can beat the West German bookies, he hopes to take the money and get the hell out of the city.

But it usually doesn't work out that way. An East Berlin bettor may make it to a West Berlin betting parlor if he's lucky, but after a fling there he usually returns to East Berlin, a poorer, sadder, but necessarily wiser man. Betting on horses has nothing to do with politics, even in a people's republic.

Everyone knows the horses are against the people.

It's hard to find an accurate tipster in East Berlin. Occasionally someone will say, "I have a friend in West Berlin who knows an Air France pilot who knows a man who goes to Enghien every day and this man knows a jockey who has a feeling about the fifth race, because of a horse named Pommes de Terre."

By the time this information is transmitted, not only is the race over, but Pommes de Terre has probably been retired and put out to stud.

But anyone who has ever visited an East German betting parlor can have nothing but admiration for an East German race enthusiast. Seated around in a dark, crowded, unfurnished room, breathing cigar smoke made from Communist Chinese tobacco, studying a racing form of French horses printed in Cologne, the East Berlin bettor, as horse bettors everywhere, is an incurable optimist. He believes that with a little luck and slightly more information, it will only be a matter of time before he'll be sitting in a plush leather chair in a West Berlin betting parlor, asking his friends: "When does the next plane leave for Paris?"

Red Food for Thought

THE thaw is on for tourists visiting East Berlin, and now when you drive through the Brandenburg Gate, the East German police salute and smile at Western visitors. Old-timers in West Berlin say they can remember when the East German police saluted in the past, and some can even remember when they smiled, but none can remember when they did both at the same time.

Another evidence of the thaw, which of course could only be temporary, is that when I inquired at one of the East Berlin tourist information centers as to the best restaurant in East Berlin, the man replied: "The Budapest. But tip the waiter beforehand, because the service is very bad."

No trip to East Berlin is complete unless you visit an East German food market and see what is available to the housewives in a "people's paradise."

The East Berlin housewife is an ardent newspaper reader—not for the advertisements, but to find out with whom East Germany has recently signed a trade treaty.

If the East Germans have just entertained a North Viet-Nam trade mission, the housewife knows that in a few months she can put dried bananas on her menu. A treaty with Guinea may bring in a large shipment of groundnuts and an editorial in favor of Iraq means the East Germans have just been stuck with a surplus of Iraqi dates.

There is a great deal of bitterness toward Albania in East Berlin now, not because of political deviationism, but because Albania recently sent East Germany a shipload of bad Albanian fish. Relations with Bulgaria have improved since the East Germans have been getting good tomato juice, but they're strained with Communist China because their friendly ally has been sending them nothing but rotting tangerines.

The Russians haven't been very helpful to the East Germans because they keep sending caviar to the capitalist powers in exchange for hard currency, instead of supplying their friends in the satellite countries.

Instead of caviar, the Russians have been giving the East Germans cheese.

It's hard for the East Germans to understand why the Russians don't give *them* the caviar and the capitalists the cheese.

The only possible explanation is that the Russians don't want to do anything at the moment to upset East-West relations.

If they can't come to an agreement on disarmament, the Russians have promised to take a harder line, and the first step in that direction would be to sell the Western bloc their Russian cheese.

Not all food in an East Berlin supermarket is imported. East Germany has had a very good herring catch this winter and if you want fish you can have herring for the asking—herring in cream, herring in tomato sauce, herring in wine sauce, herring in beer sauce, herring in smoked bacon gravy, and, for variety, kippered herring in glass jars.

Anyone who loves herring would love an East German supermarket.

Shopping in an East Berlin food store is, if you'll excuse the expression, like Russian roulette. You never know what you're going to find on the shelves or why.

But it saves the housewife the trouble of making up a daily menu and it keeps her in touch with faraway places. Where else could you go into any food store and buy as many Viet-Namese dried bananas as you want, with no questions asked?

As Long as You Fight Well

THE first recorded Olympic Games took place in 776 B.C. in what is now known as ancient Greece, but at the time was known as modern Greece. It is rumored that the games really started four hundred years before then, but no one knows who was responsible.

One theory was that it was started by a wealthy Athenian named Sam Olympics. Sam had four very fast daughters and one day he challenged a very rich Greek friend, Spyros Gabor, who also had four very fast daughters, to a relay race. The Olympic girls beat out the Gabor sisters by a length and after that the relay games in Greece were named the Olympics after them. Had the Gabor sisters won it would have been known as the World Gabor Games. As a matter of fact Spyros was so depressed by the loss he moved his family to Hungary, where nothing has been heard of them since.

So much for history.

The XVIIth Games opened in Rome to a crowd of 1,750 people and 98,250 unaccredited newspapermen. Rome waited a long time for these Olympics. Originally they were supposed to take place during the time of Emperor Nero. But the athlete who was carrying the torch from Athens slipped just as he reached the outskirts of Rome and set the whole city on fire.

Emperor Nero, a philosophical man, decided to hold a music festival instead, featuring himself on the violin.

And so Rome had to wait all these years before it could make an attempt at holding another one.

The official slogan of the Olympics, written by Pierre de Coubertin, a great high-hurdles star, is that "the most important thing in the Olympic Games is not to win but to take part, just as the most important thing in life is not to have conquered but to have fought well."

This slogan could fit the fans at the Olympic Games as well as the participants. Not every fan won on opening day, but everyone who tried to get into the giant Olympic stadium fought well.

Without even knowing it I placed first in the wrestling trials when I tried to hammer-lock an Australian who was sitting in my seat. But I lost in the finals when an Italian soda-pop salesman pinned me down on the ground trying to pass a paper cup to someone three rows above me.

Although there were not supposed to be any competitions on opening day, several were held outside the stadium. The most important event was parking, which was won by Italian President Gronchi, who parked his car in 14 seconds flat. The Americans did very poorly in this event, some of them taking as long as 3 hours and 40 minutes to find a spot. The Americans have themselves to blame for their sad performance. None of them had trained in Roman traffic, and many of the ones who participated had only two or three hours' sleep the night before.

They also were not familiar with the course which takes them to the stadium. Several were eliminated when they missed a turn in the Borghese Gardens and wound up in Milan.

But despite the poor showing of the American Olympic fans on the first day they were still expected to win many of the extra-Olympic events held during the regular Olympic session. The smart money said they would win the Italian tipping competition hands down.

They were also expected to set new world records in hotel bills.

In these two events the Russians didn't have a chance.

A Street in Rome

IF THE Battle of Waterloo was won on the playing fields of
Eton, then the battle of the 1960 Olympics was won on the
sidewalks of the Via Veneto. The Via Veneto pretends to be
a street, but it is in fact a gigantic arena, three blocks long
and seventeen motor scooters wide, where all the nonathletic
life of Rome takes place.

Along both sides of the arena are sidewalk cafés, each with
its own clientele and its own way of life. The most famous
is Doney's, next to the Excelsior Hotel, which is occupied
only by American tourists, and where, as one person put it,
"you see the people that you were on the ship with." One of
the waiters at Doney's said his one ambition in life before he
dies was to meet someone who spoke Italian.

Doney's is said to have the best cup of Italian coffee in
the world, but because it is considered tourist territory the
Italians shun it (not that they could get a table anyway)
preferring one of the other cafés.

The most successful "Italian" café on the Via Veneto is
the Café de Paris, where the *dolce vita* crowd is said to hold
forth. *Dolce vita*, which means "sweet life," has to do with
the more decadent aspects of Rome, and the people who
sit at the Café de Paris like to think they're more decadent
than anybody else.

Unfortunately, the tourists are starting to move over to the
Café de Paris, because they want to be part of the *dolce vita*
themselves, and if the trend continues, the *dolce vita* crowd
may move back to Doney's, where they wanted to sit in the
first place.

Up the street is Rosati's, the café of Roman intellectuals
and aristocracy, who have nothing but contempt for the people who sit at Doney's and the Café de Paris.

The better co-production movie deals are discussed at

Rosati's before the final lies are drawn up at the bar of the Hotel Excelsior.

Next to Rosati's is Carpano, a café owned by an Italian-American. Carpano has been getting the overflow from Rosati's and many of the intellectuals who are now sitting at Carpano tables served by Carpano waiters are so busy discussing things they think they're sitting at Rosati's.

Across the street is Jerry's, also owned by an Italian-American. Jerry's, located in front of the night club Brick Top, gets the American movie trade. There is also a café called Strega, which an Italian friend told me gets the "*dolce vita* crowd that isn't kidding."

Strega was the first café on the Via Veneto to put in reclining chairs, but so many people went to sleep in them during the afternoon that the chairs were taken away.

The American Embassy is located on the Via Veneto, but this is not an accident. It was put there for the convenience of young American girls. What happens on the Via Veneto is that a pretty or not-so-pretty American girl takes a table at a café. Then a good-looking Italian man makes a pass at her. Pretty soon she's deeply in love. A girl who can pay her own way is very much admired by the men on the Via Veneto, and eventually the girl has used up all her traveler's checks.

When those are gone, the girl then gets a refund on the return part of her plane ticket. After she spends this on her boy friend, she has nothing left and he loses interest in her. It is then that the girl turns to the American Embassy for help, and it is for this reason that it is located so close by.

Needless to say, any woman has a difficult time walking up and down the Via Veneto without being touched. One American woman who had been pinched went up to a traffic policeman on the corner and complained. The policeman asked her to point out the man who did it.

When the woman did, the policeman said: "It's all right. I know the man. He's okay."

The interesting thing about the Via Veneto is that it's a two-way street. The people at the tables are staring at the people who are walking, and the people who are walking are staring at the people at the tables. I saw one man reading his newspaper at Jerry's the other morning when a beautiful Italian girl went by. The man immediately put down his newspaper and started to applaud.

The most important thing about the Via Veneto is that it gives a chance for everyone to talk to everybody else. The other night I was sitting at Doney's next to Eva Gabor's table. An American woman stopped and said to Eva, "Aren't you Zsa Zsa Gabor?"

"No, I'm Eva," Miss Gabor said through her teeth.

"Isn't that funny," the woman said. "I just had dinner with your sister two weeks ago."

Mother Was a Lousy Sprinter

NOT everyone in Rome during the Olympics was excited about them. One person in this category was Peter Ustinov, the British actor and director, who was just putting the finishing touches on his film *Romanoff and Juliet*.

Mr. Ustinov blames his lack of interest on his early childhood, when he was a student at Mr. Gibbs's prep school in England. Ustinov's father was a Russian who worked in Germany before becoming a British citizen. His mother was French.

"It was thirty years ago," the thirty-nine-year-old actor said, "but I can still remember everything that made me hate the Olympics. It had to do with Mr. Gibbs's annual sports day. Once a year, our fathers and mothers and chauffeurs came to Mr. Gibbs's prep school for the sports day. But they weren't there just to watch us race, they had to compete themselves—the fathers against the fathers, the mothers against the mothers, and the chauffeurs against the chauffeurs. Each race was a hundred-yard dash, and naturally your standing in the school was enhanced by how well your parents and chauffeur did in the race.

"Unfortunately, we didn't have a chauffeur, and at a school like Mr. Gibbs's this was unforgivable. If you had no father it carried sympathy. If you had no chauffeur you were condemned."

"Couldn't you offer some excuse for not having a chauffeur?"

"In those days in England," Mr. Ustinov said sadly, "there was absolutely no excuse for not having a chauffeur.

"You can't imagine the anguish I went through. I begged my father—I said: 'I don't want a car, father, I just want a chauffeur.' Today, of course, you could rent one from Hertz to run in the hundred-yard dash, but in those days a rented chauffeur was not allowed to qualify. Some of the boys in our school were so rich they had enough chauffeurs to field a relay team."

"Did the chauffeurs race in uniform?"

"Always," Mr. Ustinov said, "but the one liberty they were permitted was that they were able to wear sneakers. It wasn't that I didn't have a chauffeur alone that was so humiliating, it was also that my father wouldn't run in the fathers' race. Father was a former German diplomat and he wore a monocle. He felt it was beneath his dignity to race the hundred-yard dash, and he also had a fear of losing his monocle. So while the other boys at school had their mothers, fathers, and chauffeurs to cheer on, all my marbles were on my mother, and she turned out to be a lousy sprinter."

"What was wrong?"

"Her start was very bad, and she preferred to go off from a standing position, while all the other mothers crouched. Time and time again I told my mother she would never get a good start from a standing position, but she was very stubborn and wouldn't listen. Naturally, Mother always came in last and since she was the only one I had in the competitions I had to apologize for her bad form to the other boys—a most terrible experience.

"To make matters worse the boys at Mr. Gibbs's knew my father was German and, to be unkind, they said I lost the First World War. There were only a few who were pleasant and they said that their fathers had told them that whenever they overran a German trench they found the sanitary conditions immaculate as compared to those of the French. But since I had a French mother, even this was not consoling.

"So Olympics may mean something to other people," Mr. Ustinov said, "but all they do for me is remind me of my mother puffing down the hundred-yard track, suffering from bad acceleration and trying so desperately to make up to me for the fact her husband wouldn't run and we didn't have a chauffeur."

Mr. Ustinov wiped a tear from his eye. "Maybe she was a lousy sprinter—but she was my mother."

Italians Excel in Pinching Miss Taylor

THERE were many ways to see the Olympic Games. One of the most interesting but also the most dangerous was to go to one of the events with Miss Elizabeth Taylor. Miss Taylor was there only as a spectator, and could no longer compete in the Olympics for the United States because she lost her amateur standing by signing to play Cleopatra against Marc Antony for a cool million dollars.

The actress stopped off in Rome with her husband, Mr. Eddie Fisher, and her doctor, Rex Kennemer. Although the Italians love sports, they love women more, and Miss Taylor received her share of admiration from the hot-blooded Romans.

Because of the heat she had only been attending the evening events, mostly water polo. It wasn't that Miss Taylor

was a great water-polo enthusiast. It was just that by the time she got ready, water polo was the only sport still going on.

One night I was invited to attend the water-polo matches with her, and it was quite an event—not the water polo, but going with her.

When we arrived at the swimming stadium the crowds immediately recognized her and surged forward. Helpful hands reached out and touched her and Miss Taylor shouted to Mr. Fisher: "Someone touched my chest."

"Who?" Mr. Fisher wanted to know.

All the Italians around us held up their hands to show it wasn't them.

We moved forward slowly and suddenly Miss Taylor yelled again: "Someone is pinching me."

Mr. Fisher shouted: "Who?"

"I don't know," she shouted, "I'm being pinched in the back."

"Where?" the doctor wanted to know.

"You know where," Miss Taylor said.

"Bella, bella," the Italians shouted.

Mr. Fisher yelled to me: "You protect her in the back, I'll protect her in the front, and the doc can take the flanks."

The flanks at this point were the most vulnerable and not only the Italians but players from Spain and France had joined the sport.

The scoring I figured out later went something like this. A pinch on the lower part of Miss Taylor's flanks was worth one point. On the lower part of her back was three points, and on her chest, which in Italy is the equivalent of a touchdown, was worth six points.

Since I was covering the rear I had the job of being the goalie. In a sport of this kind it is considered the toughest position on the field. Several fingers intended for Miss Taylor pinched me instead. "You're not allowed to pinch the goalie," I cried out in pain. But the officials were looking at Miss Taylor and paying no attention to me.

Slowly we made our way forward. The Italians had sent

in substitutes and Miss Taylor screamed again: "They're still pinching me."

"Walk sideways," I suggested.

But this didn't work either, and the Italians were scoring all over the place.

At this point the photographers joined in and they kept stopping us so that they could take pictures of the event—which was certainly an Olympic pinching record.

It must have been twenty-five minutes before someone finally blew a whistle. It turned out to be a policeman, and the game was over.

The final score, Mr. Fisher told me the next morning after making the tally, was 334 pinches and 12 touchdowns against the Americans, the worst beating the United States has ever taken from Italy since the Olympic Games started.

The Italians have asked for a return match but Miss Taylor refused so far to give them one. If she does she's going to have to find a new goalie, because I haven't been able to sit down since.

Conversation on a Plane

TRAVELING the way I do, I'm always running into interesting people. The other day on my way up from Rome I met a white-haired German business man. This was my end of the conversation.

"Yes, I speak English. . . . No, I'm not English, I'm American. Oh, you're German. . . . Thank you for your card. . . . Here's mine. . . . I see you're in the steel business. That must be a good business. . . . Oh, you once owned your own steel plant in Leipzig? Before the war? During the war. . . . The British and the Americans destroyed your plant? How? . . . With bombs. That's a shame. Were they big bombs? . . . Very big bombs. That really is a shame. . . . They destroyed your plant twice. You rebuilt it and then they destroyed it again. . . . That's terrible. They shouldn't have done it. I mean, after all it was your plant and . . . Were they high-flying planes or low-flying planes? . . . You couldn't tell because you were in a bomb shelter. . . . But the bombs made a lot of noise? . . . I can appreciate how you felt. . . .

"But isn't Leipzig in the Eastern zone? . . . Then you were captured by the Russians? Did they throw you in prison? . . . Only for a couple of weeks? That's too bad. I mean that's bad that they threw you in prison. . . . Did they mistreat you? They did. . . . Isn't that awful. I bet they tortured you. . . . They did! Isn't that wonderful. I mean isn't that wonderful that they didn't torture you more than two weeks. . . . Were you a member of the Nazi party? . . . Naturally, of course you weren't. . . . I'm sorry I asked. . . .

"I see. . . . All you did was make steel for the army. . . . You had to. Of course you did. . . . No, I wasn't in the Air Force. I was in the Marines. We were in the Pacific. We didn't bomb any German steel plants. . . . We wanted to . . . that is to say, we wanted to be in the European theater. Everybody during the war wanted to be some place else. . . . No, I'm not bitter about the war. I've got nothing against the Germans, particularly somebody who made steel. It isn't as if you were fighting us. . . . After all, you can make other things with steel besides guns . . . like Venetian blinds or air-conditioning units. I'll bet that's what your plant made. . . . You made steel hospital beds? There, what did I tell you! I knew you were the type of person that wouldn't make war equipment. . . . Tell me, did anyone else torture you besides the Russians? The East German Communists arrested you but didn't torture you? . . . What's wrong with them? . . . No, I mean what's their problem, I didn't mean what was wrong with them for not torturing you. . . . You'll have to excuse me, my English isn't so good.

"No, I don't speak German. I live in France. . . . Oh yes, I like it very much. . . . You had French workers working for you during the war? . . . Did they work well? . . . Not so good? . . . They work much better now. . . . I guess during the war they didn't like to work so much. . . . The French are funny that way. Put them in their own steel plant and they'll work like mad . . . but send them to a German steel plant and they'll goof off every time. . . .

"I see by your card you're still in the steel business. In West Germany. How's it going? . . . Very good. . . . That's too bad. I mean that's too bad that you can't be in the steel business in East Germany.

"I'll bet you're furious at the Americans and British for destroying your plant. . . . You're not any more because now they're among your best customers? And you say your business is even bigger than it was before the war? . . . That's wonderful, really, really wonderful. . . .

"No, stewardess, I don't want any lunch. For some reason I just lost my appetite."

7. Ça C'est Show Biz

You Wrote the Book: Now
See the Picture

SOME time ago I wrote a book called *A Gift From the Boys*, which I had the good fortune to sell to the movies. At the time, Cary Grant announced he was going to play in it and you can't imagine how happy everyone in the family was, except the children who were too young to know who Cary Grant was.

Well, time passed and the other day I met someone from the company, who informed me the book had been made into a picture.

"That's funny," I said, "I don't remember reading anything about *A Gift From the Boys* being made into a film."

The man laughed and said: "Oh, we're not calling it *A Gift From the Boys*. We're calling it *Surprise Package*. *A Gift From the Boys* sounds too much like *Suddenly Last Summer*."

He could see I was visibly disappointed. "But don't worry, everything else has been left intact. All we did was take your novel and put it on the screen."

"How is Grant as a Sicilian gangster?"

"Oh, didn't anyone tell you? Grant's not in it. Yul Brynner is playing the deportee. And we've changed him from a Sicilian to a Greek. Brynner looks more like a Greek than a Sicilian. Frankly, he doesn't look like either. If we really wanted to do it right we should have made it in Mongolia."

"Well," I said, "I guess there is no harm changing the locale. Who plays the Gift from the boys?"

"We threw that idea out the first day. There is no gift from the boys. Mitzi Gaynor plays a girl friend of the gangster, but as long as we changed the title there was no sense making her a gift any more. Noel Coward gives a wonderful performance as the king."

"What king?" I asked, startled.

"You know, the king—oh, that's right, you don't know the king. We've added a king to the story. It's terribly funny and saves the picture."

"Is the gangster sent back to the town where he was born?" I asked.

"No, we threw that out the first day."

"Does he organize the fishermen into smuggling cigarettes?" I wanted to know.

"Heavens, no," he said. "We threw that out the first day too. We did want to keep the fishing boats, but we couldn't because we threw out the fishermen. You see what we were up against."

"It must have been hard," I said sympathetically. "Is the bodyguard still in the picture?"

"We liked him so much we didn't throw him out until the second day. He was a very good character. But you can't use everything in the book."

"How does the kidnaping scene work?" I wanted to know. He looked puzzled.

"What kidnaping?"

"You remember, when the gangster is kidnaped by Mondello, the bandit, and held for ransom?"

"Oh yes, I almost forgot about that." He made a gesture with his thumb.

"The first day?" I asked.

He nodded sadly. "The first hour of the first day."

"Well, does the girl get kidnaped by Mondello?"

"Not in this picture," he replied.

"I guess you've made a different story," I said.

"Now, that's not true. There are lots of things from the book in the movie. You know the policeman in your story that has his bicycle stolen by the Mafia?"

"Yes," I said excitedly.

"Well, he's still in the picture, only we changed him and

made him the chief of police. But we had to throw out the business about the stolen bicycle.

"And," he continued, "you know the café in the square where everyone meets? Well, it's now part of the hotel, but anyone who has read the book will know it's the café. Nico March hangs around the café in the picture just as he does in the book."

"Wait a minute," I cried. "Who's Nico March?"

"The lead character."

"But my lead character was named Frank Bartlett."

The man seemed to be losing his patience. "You apparently don't know anything about movies. If we had to hold on to every little detail we'd never be able to adapt anything for the screen. You should be grateful your book has been made into a picture by people who loved the story and only changed things to help it."

I apologized for even questioning him on it. "After all, it's only my first novel," I said tearfully, "and I don't know anything about motion pictures."

"Don't feel too bad," he said, putting his arm around my shoulder. "Even Faulkner doesn't understand why they do the things they do with his books. All book writers have a blind spot when it comes to their own work."

The Latest Thing in Flying

I HAD a Thanksgiving lunch at Chez Louis with Shelley Berman, the American comedian, and his wife. Louis had promised us a typical American Thanksgiving meal and it was as typically American as he could get. We had chopped chicken liver to start with, turkey *without* dressing, apple sauce, potato salad, and rice pudding.

The meal made the three of us homesick—homesick for Czechoslovakia, that is.

Mr. Berman is a very successful young American comic who has two best-selling talk records which have catapulted him into stardom. One of his "bits" had to do with a ride on a commercial airplane, and stewardesses and pilots have been going out of their minds ever since, when passengers quote Mr. Berman's routine to them.

But Mr. Berman, like most comics, is always searching for new material and he told me at lunch that he had just read an item in *Newsweek* that a major air line is considering a deal to show Hollywood films on board its planes while they are in flight. The sound for the films would be piped via earphones.

"This will open an entire new era for flying," Mr. Berman predicted. "In future when people want to book a reservation to Europe, the first question they will ask is 'What's playing?' "

"I can hear the pilot speaking now. 'This is your captain—Spyros Skouras. Our playing time is two hours and thirteen minutes and we will have a fifteen-minute intermission at Montreal. Our negative is clear and we will be showing thirty-five thousand feet. If you look on the left side of the screen you will see Henry Fonda, and if you look on the right you will see Audrey Hepburn. Our alternate route is over Tony Perkins and Ingrid Bergman. Shortly after take-off we will be serving popcorn. Please fasten your eyeballs and no smoking during the coming attractions.' "

Mr. Berman felt that in order to justify the difference in price the air lines would show the films in color in first class on a large screen, and in black and white on a small screen in tourist class.

Air France would naturally show French films and therefore many of their flights would be "For adults only."

The nonscheduled air lines would only be permitted to show art films.

The jets would have first crack at new films and the prop planes would probably be given such pictures as *The Jazz Singer*.

Mr. Berman thought that the new innovation would change everyone's living habits.

"Can't you see a guy coming home from the office and his wife complaining: 'I'm so bored. You always come home and plop in a chair and take your shoes off. You never take me out any more.'

"The husband replies: 'Okay, okay. What's showing at Pan American tonight?'

"The wife picks up a PAA plane schedule. 'The 901 to Rome is featuring *The Apartment,* the 506 to Bangkok is playing *The World of Suzie Wong* and the 107 to Hong Kong is playing *Ben Hur,* but if we want to see the chariot race we have to change at Tokyo.'

"The husband replies: 'I've got a big day tomorrow, let's go to Rome. How much is it for a reserved seat?'

"The wife refers to another part of the schedule: 'It's $1,064.90 round-trip but that includes a newsreel and Bugs Bunny cartoon. If we want unreserved seats it's $532.45 but there are no short subjects.'

"The husband decides to get reserved seats. The next day they ask their best friends, 'Did you see *The Apartment?*' And the friends reply, 'We decided to go to Hawaii instead.' "

Some Like Their Crow Hot

MR. BILLY WILDER, the director of *Some Like It Hot* and *The Apartment,* has bought the French play *Irma La Douce* to make as his next comedy. *Irma La Douce* is the story of a French prostitute whose lover is very jealous of her other affairs. Irma's dream is to have one steady client who will support her and her lover. The lover disguises himself as a rich old man and makes the proposition that if Irma remains loyal to him, he will give her ten thousand francs a day.

Irma agrees, and that evening she gives her lover the

ten thousand francs the old man has given her. The next
day the lover disguised as the old man gives Irma the same
ten thousand francs and that evening she gives it to her
lover. The lover has his girl to himself and the same ten
thousand francs keeps making the cycle.

Unfortunately the lover, who also has to work scrubbing
floors to support the two, is getting tired of playing the
dual role and he becomes very jealous of the old man and
"kills" him.

It is from this plot that Mr. Wilder must make his movie.

"Who is going to play Irma?" I asked Mr. Wilder.

"I don't know yet," he said. "Jack Lemmon will play the
lover, but I haven't decided yet on Irma. It could be Brigitte
Bardot, Elizabeth Taylor, Shirley MacLaine, or Marilyn Monroe, but don't put them in any order, or one of them will
think I have a preference at this stage."

"I can appreciate your wanting Miss Taylor, Miss Mac-
Laine, or Miss Bardot, but it seems to me after *Some Like It
Hot* you vowed you'd never make another picture with Miss
Monroe. As a matter of fact, I didn't think after what you
said about her that you were even on speaking terms."

"We made up at the Khrushchev luncheon at Twentieth
Century-Fox. The FBI asked all of us to be there at noon
for security reasons, and Marilyn, who flew in from New
York, not only showed up on time but was twenty minutes
early. This was the first time I had ever seen her early for
anything, and I was so thrown by it I threw my arms around
her and we made up on the spot.

"I vowed then that if I did another picture with her I'd
hire Khrushchev to hang around the set so she'd show up
on time."

"But," I said, passing the crow to Mr. Wilder, "you said
you would *never, never* make another picture with Miss
Monroe."

Mr. Wilder took a big bite and, after spitting out the
feathers, replied: "I said I would never smoke again, and
I'm still smoking. A man has a right to change his mind."

"But you said you had to wait on the set hours and hours

for her and then you weren't sure whether she would show up or not."

"Exactly," Mr. Wilder said, taking another bite. "But we didn't waste those hours. We played poker, I managed to read *War and Peace*, *Les Misérables*, and *Hawaii*, and we all got wonderful suntans. The extras made twice as much money as they expected, and, while it might have taken slightly longer to make the film, we did get to know one another so much better."

"But," I said, "you said, at the time, when she did show up she never knew her lines."

"That's the beauty of working with Monroe," he said. "She's not a parrot. Anyone can remember lines, but it takes a real artist to come on the set and not know her lines and give the performance she did."

"But how can you reconcile the statements you made about her in the past with your decision to consider her for the *Irma La Douce* role?"

Mr. Wilder started chewing on one of the crow's legs. "When I gave the interview I had just finished the picture and I was speaking under duress and the influence of barbiturates and I was suffering from high blood pressure and I had been brainwashed. Now that I can see it in a clear light I realize that she was worth it all."

There was nothing left of the crow but the beak, but Mr. Wilder picked that up. "Besides, we'll be making *Irma La Douce* in Paris, and if I do use Marilyn Monroe and if she does show up late on the set, we won't be wasting our time, because we can all learn how to paint."

A Question of Insurance

As I once mentioned, Twentieth Century-Fox was having a row with Lloyd's of London over how much insurance was involved because Elizabeth Taylor became ill and *Cleopatra* had to be postponed. It is estimated that between one and three million dollars was at stake and negotiations have been going on in London for several years between the interested parties.

At one point in the negotiations, Miss Taylor's agent, Kurt Frings, flew over to London from Hollywod to protect his client's interests. Before leaving, Mr. Frings bought a five-hundred-dollar cashmere suit as he heard London was very chilly at that time of the year. Mr. Frings also represents Audrey Hepburn, so five hundred dollars is not too much to spend for a suit. As a matter of fact it's just about right.

The first thing Mr. Frings did when he arrived at his hotel in London was send the suit out to be pressed. A few hours later the valet returned to inform Mr. Frings that unfortunately someone had burned a hole in the sleeve of the coat of his suit and he was very sorry.

The hole, it turned out, was the size of an iron and some-one had tried to sew up the burn without any success.

Mr. Frings was crestfallen until a friend told him the hotel was insured against such accidents, and so the two of them went to see the manager who confirmed it and said he would notify the insurance company immediately.

The agent then went off to have insurance discussions with Spyros Skouras and Lloyd's of London.

Two mornings later two men in bowler hats appeared with umbrellas, knocked at the door of his hotel room, and said they were from the insurance company.

Mr. Frings thought they had come to discuss Miss Taylor's insurance problem.

"We came about the suit," one of the insurance men said.

"We're not going to sue," Mr. Frings said. "Only Skouras can sue."

"We're happy to hear that," the other one said. "Who is Mr. Skouras?"

"He is the president of Twentieth Century-Fox."

"Oh, then it is his suit?"

"What suit?"

The men looked at each other. "The cashmere suit."

"No, that's my suit."

"Did someone burn a hole in Mr. Skouras's suit also?"

"No," Mr. Frings said, "Mr. Skouras is suing about something else."

Once they got this straightened out the two men started to question Mr. Frings about his cashmere suit.

They seemed very suspicious that anyone would pay five hundred dollars for a cashmere suit, but Mr. Frings insisted he could produce a bill from his Beverly Hills tailor to prove it.

"All right," one of the men said. "Let's assume you did pay five hundred dollars for the suit. Are you sure it was a new suit?"

"Of course it was a new suit. I had never worn it."

The other man jumped in. "If you had never worn it, why did you send it out to be pressed?"

"Because it was wrinkled in my luggage."

"Why didn't you just hang it out on a hanger?" the other man asked.

"Because I always have my suits pressed. I'm a very important agent. If I didn't have my suits pressed I wouldn't be serving my clients. What producer would want Elizabeth Taylor or Audrey Hepburn for a picture if they were represented by an agent in a wrinkled suit?"

The two insurance men started to look uncomfortable.

"Perhaps," one of them suggested, "we could put a new sleeve in the suit."

"It can't be done," Mr. Frings said. "I called my tailor in California and he said he didn't have any more of the material."

"You *called* your tailor in California about your suit?" the insurance man asked in a shocked voice.

"Of course," Mr. Frings said. "I always call him when someone burns a hole in my suit."

"What did he tell you?"

"He told me to start a suit."

"What kind of a suit?"

"A lawsuit."

Both gentlemen got up.

"We think we have all the information we need," one of them said. "We will have to take the suit with us."

"What are you going to do with it?" Mr. Frings demanded.

"Mr. Frings, the suit is ours now, and we don't have to tell you what we're going to do with it. But we'll make an exception in your case. We're going to show the suit to our colleagues, because otherwise no one, but no one, in the office would believe us."

Advice to Writers

MR. IRVING WALLACE recently wrote a novel based on a female sex survey in southern California. The book is called *The Chapman Report,* named after a fictitious Dr. Chapman who probes into the sex lives of six "typical" American women. To nobody's surprise the book was on many of the best-seller lists. Darryl F. Zanuck bought it for a film, and there will be a pocket-book printing of 4,000,000 copies.

If all goes well and people don't lose their interest in the subject matter between now and next year, Mr. Wallace could make a million dollars on his book.

One of the reasons Mr. Wallace is now in Paris is that with his present tax setup his accountant insisted he had to take the trip.

"I was very happy in southern California," he said. "After writing four other novels I finally hit pay dirt, and I wanted to enjoy it. But my accountant said I had to get out in the world and start writing off some of the money against taxes. 'You can't just sit around and let the government take your money,' he warned me. 'You've got to get off your back until you've written off a good percentage of the book.' So here I am, trying to use up the royalties."

Mr. Wallace said an author goes through several stages in life. In the first stage, when he is young and unpublished, he sits in front of Paris cafés or in Greenwich Village espresso bars discussing Proust, Stendhal, Joyce, and Gide. He spends the better part of the day talking characters, plot, subplot, and motivation.

"It's only after an author is published that he forgets about Proust, Stendhal, Joyce, and Gide. Instead he talks about Random House, Simon and Schuster, Doubleday, William Morris, MCA, and *The Saturday Review*. A really successful author has even more interesting things to talk about than that."

I decided to interview Mr. Wallace in the typical author-book interviewer style.

"Mr. Wallace, what are you working on now?"

"I hope to get a tax spread, and I'm trying to work out ways of leaving some of my money to my children."

"Could you tell me as a successful author how you work?"

"I have four lawyers, an accountant, and an agent. In the morning I get up around eight o'clock, go to my den, and call up the lawyers. They tell me if I'm being sued by anybody or whether I should sue anyone. Then I call up my accountant, who gives me a new plot for the Internal Revenue Department. My agent calls me and we discuss the next thirty books he's committed me to write."

"Who are the writers you admire the most?"

"Irving Stone, who has dealt with foreign rights magnificently, Emily Hahn, for her fresh concept of handling travel expenses, Jerome Weidman, who has been in the vanguard of the new approach to copyright infringement and who has discovered more new legal talent than any writer of our time, Gerold Frank, who has the longest tax spread of any writer I know, and ex-President Eisenhower, who changed the law for twenty minutes in regard to author's royalties being considered capital gains and made a million dollars."

"What do you advise a writer to read?"

"*The Wall Street Journal, The Kiplinger Report, Barron's*, and *Dow-Jones*."

"Do you find writing is a lonely business?"

"Yes, particularly after the stock market closes and you

can't get any reactions to your quotations. You can talk to your broker, but when it comes right down to investing your money, you have to do it yourself."

"Some writers are painfully sensitive to criticism. Are you?"

"It depends. I got 5 per cent of the gross on the film of *The Chapman Report*, but James Michener got 10 per cent of the gross for *Hawaii*. My wife has been very critical of me for this deal, and naturally I'm sensitive about it too. But usually I don't pay any attention to the critics."

"What is your advice to young writers?"

"Learn the difference between net and gross, don't sell the television rights at the same time you sell the movie rights, always try to get a large advance on pocket books, and make your publisher advertise."

"But what about characterization, plot, and content of the book?"

Mr. Wallace replied, "Huh?"

Astronauts Ahoy!

THE news that Russian Major Yuri Gagarin went into space and back again was greeted with joy in some circles and trepidation in others. Among those caught flat-footed were several independent motion-picture producers in Hollywood who were working on pictures such as *Space Pilot, First Man Into Outer Space*, and *Astronauts Ahoy*.

Although I wasn't out in Hollywood when the news of Gagarin's flight was announced I can imagine the spot most producers were in and I can also imagine a telephone conversation between a Hollywood producer and his writer.

The producer says: "Hello, Harry. Did you hear the radio?"

The writer replies: "No, Sam, I've been working on the script."

"How's it going?"

"Pretty good, Sam. I think we're home free."

"Well, look, Harry, there's a few minor changes I want to make in the script."

"Sure, Sam, what are they?"

"You know in our story we have this American space pilot who falls in love with a Russian girl?"

"Yeh."

"Well, I want to make it a Russian space pilot falling in love with an American girl."

"But . . ."

"Don't argue, Harry. I've got a lot of money tied up in this project. Now you remember the scene we had where Khrushchev is pounding his shoe against the desk when he hears an American's been the first man into space."

"Yeh."

"Well, take it out."

"What do you mean take it out? It's the best scene in the picture."

"Harry, boy, just take it out."

"I don't understand, Sam."

"You will, but only after the changes. Now read me the first thing the hero says when he gets out of his spaceship."

"He says: 'I couldn't have done it without my mother, and all the wonderful American people who believed in me.' "

"That's the line, Harry. I want to change it."

"Change it to what?"

"I want him to say: 'I wish to report to the Communist Party and the government and personally to Nikita Sergeivich Khrushchev that the landing was normal. I feel fine and I have no injuries or bruises.' Have you got that?"

"I've got it, Sam, but are you sure that's what a man who has been in space would say?"

"I'm sure, Harry, I'm sure."

"Well, what other changes do you want to make?"

"You know the big scene at Times Square, when it's announced that our guy has made it, with all the tumult and noise."

"Right."

"Well, keep it in, but change it to Red Square."

"Okay, Sam. It's your picture."

"What are you working on now?"

"The final scene when the guy goes on Ed Sullivan's TV show and he's reunited with the girl and Ed gives them a completely new furnished house as a wedding present."

"Well, scrap it. We'll keep the TV setting, but Ed will have to give them a co-operative farm instead."

"Gee, Sam, I don't know if Bill Holden will approve of all these changes."

"Don't worry about him, Harry. I don't think Bill Holden's right for the part any more."

"Then who are we going to get?"

"I've got a call in for Yul Brynner now."

A Serious Festival

THE international film festival in Cannes has changed its character during the years. It's more serious now—the gin rummy stakes are higher, there are more wives than girls on the beach, and there are fewer movie stars around to distract the photographers from taking pictures of each other.

Percentagewise, the film festival attendance breaks down as follows: 64 per cent is made up of producers who are trying to raise money for a co-production film; 33 per cent is made up of producers who have already made a co-production film, but can't sell it; 12 per cent is made up of agents trying to sell the producers who have no money literary properties they don't represent; 25 per cent is made up of film-trade magazine editors who are trying to sell advertisement space to the producers to announce pictures they have no intention of making; and 5 per cent is made up of film distributors who claim they can't sell a film festival picture to save their lives, but they would be interested in anything that has been banned from the festival for censorship reasons.

If this comes to more than 100 per cent, don't be disturbed. All of us have to work on a profit down here.

The lack of movie stars has been the main complaint at Cannes. Sophia Loren was here because her film *Two Women* was in the festival and she had a good chance of winning the prize for the best actress. Gina Lollobrigida was here. She doesn't have a film in the festival, but Sophia Loren does, if you know what I mean.

Sidney Poitier was here for *Raisin in the Sun* and Tony Perkins, Ingrid Bergman, and Yves Montand arrived to attend the performance of their entry, *Goodbye Again.*

We almost lost these three stars through a clerical error on the part of my hotel. Mr. Anatole Litvak, the producer and director of *Goodbye Again,* arrived at the Carlton Hotel in advance of his group, to discover he not only didn't have a suite at the hotel—he didn't even have a room.

When he discovered this, he decided to withdraw his film from the festival, because there is no sense bringing a picture to the festival if you have to sleep on the beach.

The festival authorities were naturally upset, particularly since they didn't want to lose Miss Bergman, Tony Perkins, and Yves Montand.

For three hours it was touch and go. For the want of a hotel room, three movie stars were lost. Panic reigned through the festival hall. Finally Mr. Litvak was found accommodations (someone had been to the casino in the afternoon and was forced to move for lack of funds) and *Goodbye Again* was back in the competition.

It's these little things that make a festival exciting. You never know who's going to show up without a hotel room.

There is a great deal of serious business going on at a film festival, thanks to the wives of the producers and distributors.

In order to get away from their wives, the men make business appointments with each other to discuss deals they have no intention of making.

Many of these meetings take place on the beach, on a yacht, or at the casino, and the only thing that's ever exchanged is a deck of cards. The wives are very understanding and they keep out of their husbands' way by going to Cartier's and Van Cleef and Arpels' to kill the time. The wives believe you can always see a good film, but diamonds last forever.

A strange thing has happened at the festival this year. In previous years starlets and aspiring actresses used to show up by the hundreds. But this year there seem to be very few, hardly any. I am not just saying this because I left my wife in Paris and she will be reading this—but because it's true. Just as true as that it's been snowing here for four days.

Waiting for Wiener

I HAVEN'T been to an international film festival in years, and so I decided to pay a visit to the XIVth Festival, which is taking place in Cannes on the sunny Riviera.

Nothing seems to have changed since the last time I was here. There are the same familiar producer and director faces, the same free-loading newspapermen and women, and although they must have been changed, they look like the same starlets posing for the same photographers on the same beach in the same positions they took five years ago.

A film festival is like a state fair—everybody knows everybody else, but nobody knows anybody's else's name.

One man whom I have known for years, though I'm not sure where from, dashed up to me in the lobby of the Carlton Hotel, where most of the daytime action at the festival takes place, and, after shaking my hand vigorously, said: "Guess who's here?"

"Who?" I said to the man, not wanting to mention that I was too busy trying to guess his name.

"Peter," the man said.

"No kidding," I replied. "When did he get here?"

"Yesterday," the man said.

"That's great," I said.

"We'll get together, the three of us," he promised.

"Swell," I said. "It will be good to see Peter again."

The man waved and walked away, leaving me with not only the problem of who he was, but who the hell Peter was as well.

While I was mulling this over, a young lady came up and said: "You don't remember me, do you?"

"Of course I do," I said, crinkling my brow.

"I work for Jack Wiener."

"Sure, that's who you work for," I agreed. "How's good old Jack?"

"He's fine," she said. "Will you be here a few minutes?"

"Yes, I think so," I said.

"Well, will you tell Jack to wait for me? I'll be right back."

"Certainly," I said. I didn't have the heart to tell her I didn't know what Jack Wiener looked like.

But I was lucky because five minutes later a close friend came by and, since he had his name sewn on his tennis shirt, I knew it was Alain Bernheim.

"Do you know Jack Wiener?" I asked.

"Sure," Bernheim said. "He does publicity at Columbia pictures."

"Well, wait in the lobby with me a few minutes because I have a message for him from the girl who works for him."

"I can't wait long," he warned.

"Don't worry," I said. "She said she'd be back in a few minutes."

It was 12:15 in the afternoon and both of us took our stations.

Fritz Loewe, the composer of *My Fair Lady*, came by at 12:30, and said to us: "Why don't you come out to my yacht for lunch?"

"I'd like to," I said honestly, "but I'm waiting for Jack Wiener."

"Well, maybe some other time," Loewe said and wandered off with six beautiful girls.

Around 1:00, Mrs. Bernheim came down and said to Mr. Bernheim: "Let's go down to the beach and have a swim."

"I'd like to, darling, but I've got an important meeting with Jack Wiener," Bernheim replied.

About 1:30 both of us were getting hungry.

"Why don't you eat first," Bernheim suggested, "and then when you're finished, I'll eat."

"That won't work," I said, "because you don't know the girl who works for Jack, so if she comes back, you can't tell her Wiener never showed up, and if Wiener shows up while you're eating, I won't recognize him."

"That's good thinking," Bernheim said. "We both better wait."

At 2:30 Richard Widmark asked me to have a drink with him.

"Any other time," I said, "but first I have to see Jack Wiener and tell him something."

At 3:30 Gina Lollobrigida arrived and the lobby was bedlam. Photographers were punching each other, people were standing on chairs trying to see her, autograph-seekers were jammed five deep, and we were taking quite a beating.

"We'll never see Wiener in this crowd," Bernheim shouted.

"Stand on my shoulders," I yelled. And Bernheim climbed on my shoulders to get a better view of the crowd. "Do you see him?" I asked.

"No," Mr. Bernheim replied.

But one of the photographers handed him a camera and asked him to take some pictures for him.

A half-hour later the lobby cleared out and we found ourselves a couple of chairs to sit in.

"We might as well be comfortable while we wait," I said.

"That's for sure," Mr. Bernheim agreed.

Around 6:00 the lobby started filling up and we had to stand again. At 6:15 we were getting discouraged, but then Bernheim met a friend named George Marton.

"Do you know Jack Wiener?" he asked him.

"Of course," Marton said.

"Well," said Bernheim, "will you tell him when he comes in the lobby that his girl will be right back?"

"Certainly," Marton said.

Later on I was having a drink with Bernheim on the terrace of the hotel.

"That was a pretty dirty trick you played on Marton," I said.

"It's all right," Bernheim replied. "He said he didn't want to see the movie tonight anyway."

Goodby to Bygones

I HAVE a friend named Cy Howard, from Hollywood, who just arrived in Paris. Mr. Howard, a screen and television writer, was formerly married to Gloria Grahame, the screen actress, but they've been divorced for some time. He almost got married again recently and he told me all about it.

"In order for you to appreciate the story, I must start at the beginning," he told me. "A few years ago I decided to forgive and forget and make my peace with the Germans. On racial questions, Hitler and I never saw eye to eye, and it took me a long time to get over it. But finally I decided I was being ridiculous about the whole thing and, to show that bygones were bygones, I decided to buy a Mercedes-Benz. In this way I was not only showing a mature attitude, but I was also buying one of the best cars on the road.

"I must say the Mercedes was all I hoped it would be and for a while I was very happy. But I had to own two cars because my mother has always refused to let bygones be bygones, and if I showed up at her house in a German car, it would have been too much for her.

"I kept it a secret from her for six months, but one day she saw me driving down Sunset Boulevard in it and that night she said to me: 'What were you doing driving in a German car?'

"I didn't have the heart to tell her I owned it, so I said: 'Mama, my other car broke down, so I borrowed the Mercedes from a friend.'

"She said: 'Why couldn't you have borrowed a Jaguar, or a Citroen? After all we've been through, I never thought I'd see my son driving down Sunset Boulevard in a Mercedes-Benz!'

"Well, after that, the guilt about my mother was so strong I never really enjoyed the car.

"Because I owned a German car it led me to a German film star who was trying to get work in Hollywood. She was beautiful, she spent her spare hours cooking for me and cleaning the house; she always called me Liebchen and when she had nothing else to do she polished my Mercedes.

"We were very happy together and I was even thinking of possibly getting married again. As long as I had a German car, I thought, I might as well have a German wife.

"But one day I turned on the television set and there on the screen was the Eichmann trial. Frieda was cleaning the house and calling me Liebchen, but I was too fascinated listening to the testimony.

"Then she said: 'Liebchen, could I take the Mercedes to the studio? I am going to try out for the biggest part of my career.'

"I was in such a state of shock watching the Eichmann trial I muttered 'Okay' and she dashed out of the house.

"Two hours later I was still watching the trial when I heard the Mercedes pull up and the door slam. Frieda rushed into the house and she was very excited. 'Liebchen, Liebchen,' she cried as she put her arms around me, 'I've got the part—the biggest part of my career.'

" 'That's wonderful,' I said. 'What part is it?'

"Frieda said: 'I'm going to play Mrs. Eichmann in a new movie they're going to make about him.'

"I calmly went to the TV set and turned it off, then I walked to the door and calmly opened it. Then I said in my calmest voice: 'Get out and take the car with you.'

"As Frieda left she turned to me and protested: 'But Liebchen, I'm going to play the part sympathetically.' "

8. *Le Reste Sans Titre*

The Students Are Restless

I MET an old friend of mine, Nunnally Johnson, the American writer and producer, who is now living in London. Mr. Johnson seemed a little depressed and I asked him what the trouble was. "I just received a letter," he said, "from my daughter, who goes to college in Providence, Rhode Island, and she said she was very tired because she had been picketing a five-and-ten-cent store all day. It was one of a chain that wouldn't serve Negroes at lunch counters in the South.

"I was very upset and wrote back asking her what she had against colored people that she would want them to eat the kind of food they serve in a five-and-ten? Did she want them to get indigestion too? I told her that this whole question of Negroes eating at lunch counters in the South could not be resolved by picketing in the North. The best way of handling it would be to take one token Negro up to the counter of a five-and-ten and serve him the day's special, which would probably be a chocolate-covered tuna-fish sandwich."

Mr. Johnson said he couldn't understand what was getting into students these days.

"All over the world students are demonstrating and protesting, and the question is, when do they get any work done?

"When I was a kid the Big Man on Campus was the fellow who made the eighty-yard run for a touchdown. Today the Big Man on Campus is the fellow who can overturn a Buick with Jim Hagerty in it.

"The only thing the kids seem to want to study these days is geology. Once they understand the stratas and different kinds of rocks, they go out on field trips and start throwing them at prime ministers.

245

"Even the cheers have changed. I remember in college going out into the streets and shouting:

>Hey, hey, hey.
>Who's okay?
>We're okay.
>Win, win, win.

"Now the kids go out into the streets and shout:

>Hey, hey, hey.
>Who's okay?
>Nobody, nobody.
>Resign, resign, resign."

Mr. Johnson said even the attitude toward athletic scholarships is changing.

"But Scotty turned it down. He said he had a better offer day when a stranger came up and said he was a scout from the University of Tokyo. He offered him a scholarship and said: 'If you can throw a football that way, can you imagine what you could do with a Molotov cocktail?' He offered the boy a four-year education and promised to throw in a gas mask.

"But Scotty turned it down. He said he had a better offer from the University of Mexico. They offered him four years of education, a steel helmet, and free laundry service for his protest banners.

"I don't know what's going to happen to the world in 1975, based on the Class of 1960. I can just see a doctor cutting open a patient but not knowing how to sew him up again, because on the day they taught *that*, he was marching on the American Embassy in Cambodia.

"I wouldn't be surprised in fifteen years to read of a bridge collapsing because the engineer who built it was responsible for overthrowing the South Korean government.

"Maybe parents are responsible for it all," Mr. Johnson said. "We aren't so concerned any more if our kids graduate or not—we just don't want them to jump bail."

Crime Pays Better

I HAVE received a letter from an inmate of a state prison in America who says he is getting out in a month, after serving three years, and wants to become a journalist when he is released. He has asked me how he can go about it. Usually I don't bother to answer this kind of letter, but in this case I think I should, because since this man has paid his debt to society there is no sense in his going back to a life of crime, which is exactly what will happen if he becomes a newspaperman.

Dear 189654,

Thank you for your letter. You have asked me how you become a newspaperman and it's very hard to know what to tell you.

First you have to steal a typewriter.

Then you swipe some paper from the copy desk. You put the paper into the typewriter and then you start committing perjury. When you finish the article you turn it over to a copyreader who proceeds to murder everything you've written. When the final story appears in the newspaper you won't recognize it, and you're ready to assault everyone in the office.

The next day the person you wrote the story about calls up and says you're a miserable horse thief. You protest that you're innocent and the guilty one is the guy on the desk. The person says you ought to be locked up for writing a story like that and if he ever sees you again he'll shoot you.

You go see the managing editor to protest the way they manhandled your copy. He says: "You got no rights here. You're still on trial."

"But," you say, "I've got a right to defend myself."

"You're holding me up." The managing editor scowls. "Now beat it before you break my heart."

You go to a bar to try to forget and you run into a press agent who buys you a drink. Now you owe him a favor. Then he buys you another drink and you owe him two favors. Then he bribes you with a lunch. Finally he blackmails you into doing a story on his client.

Once he hooks you with one story there is no escape, and you become an accomplice in every one of his crimes.

One press agent leads to another press agent and one lunch leads to another lunch. Pretty soon you're depending on handouts and can't work unless you've got one every day. Then the day comes when you don't have one, and you break into a cold sweat and start shaking and your teeth start chattering. You can't work, you can't do anything. You go see a pusher but he says he's out, and then you start screaming. You'll do anything to get a press release, anything. The press agents know it and that's when they move in with their mimeograph machines and feed you what they want to.

But, 189654, the real reason I'd advise you against going into the newspaper business is because there is going to come a day, as it must to all newspapermen, when you get your first pay check. And when you see how much a newspaperman gets paid, there's going to be nothing left for you to do but go out and stick up a gasoline station.

All things considered, I'd advise you to go straight and become an executive for one of the big American electrical companies.

Great Tales of Courage

COURAGE is not something that only takes place in time of war. It is, in fact, much more difficult to be courageous in times of peace. But peacetime heroes never receive their true recognition. The following are true stories of men who have proved themselves above and beyond the call of duty. Each act was witnessed by two other people and the records of the incidents are available in the file in the Library of Congress.

Milton Stevens, a mild thirty-four-year-old advertising man, was sitting in his living room in Bay Shore, Long Island, on the evening of May 12, 1959, watching television when the phone rang. Stevens picked up the phone and a voice said:

"This is Anne McCarthy. Are you kids doing anything next Thursday night?"

Stevens replied: "No, we're not."

"Well," Mrs. McCarthy said, "would you and Ruth like to come over to our house for dinner?"

Stevens, without hesitation, said: "No."

A second outstanding tale of courage took place in Paris on July 2, 1960. An American tourist named Blake Edwards went with his wife up to the Flea Market where she said she wanted to buy some antiques. They entered a shop and his wife started pricing some lamps. There was one in particular she liked and she asked the man how much it was.

The shop owner said: "One hundred francs."

"How much is that in dollars?" his wife asked.

"Twenty dollars."

His wife started to haggle. "Oh, I could never afford that."

Mr. Edwards popped in immediately: "She can, too. She has plenty of money."

On December 12, 1958, Mr. Robert Parrish of Los Angeles, California, attended a party at the home of a friend in Beverly Hills, California. At the party were writers, directors, and people of the movie world. A literary discussion started and one of the screen writers at the party said to Mr. Parrish: "Have you ever read William Faulkner's *Sanctuary*?"

Mr. Parrish replied: "No, I have never read anything by William Faulkner."

Mr. and Mrs. Irving Lazar, of Brooklyn, New York, returned to the United States June 8, 1960, after their first trip to Europe, where they visited England, France, Spain, Italy,

Switzerland, and Monte Carlo. On their first evening back they were invited to the home of their best friends, Mr. and Mrs. Harry Kurnitz.

As soon as dinner was over, Mrs. Kurnitz said: "Now tell us about your trip to Europe."

Mr. Lazar said: "We'd rather not. Could we watch television instead?"

On October 12, 1959, Mr. and Mrs. Raymond Kahme met their old friends Mr. and Mrs. Michael Mindlin on the corner of Fifth Avenue and Fifty-ninth Street. The Mindlins had just become grandparents for the first time.

Mr. Mindlin took out his wallet and said: "Would you like to see a photo of her?"

Mr. Kahme replied: "No, thanks. We've seen pictures of grandchildren before."

But in all the annals of civilian courage, none could take the place of Mr. Robert Nugent, of Chicago, Illinois. Mr. Nugent went to a three-star French restaurant on May 16, 1960, and ordered a sumptuous meal, including a duck à l'orange. After a half-hour of preparation the waiter presented the sizzling duck on a silver platter. Mr. Nugent looked at it and said: "No, that's not what I had in mind. I think I'll have scrambled eggs instead."

For his courage Mr. Nugent was awarded the Civilian Medal of Honor—posthumously.

He Married an American

I HAVE talked to several American girls who have been married to Frenchmen, e.g., Dorian Leigh, Suzy Parker, and Jean Seberg (the last two are now in the process of getting divorced), but I've never talked to a Frenchman married to an American—at least not for the record.

I had the pleasant experience yesterday, when I lunched with the French stage and screen actor Claude Dauphin.

"As far as I know, I'm the only Frenchman married to an American thirty years younger than he is who lives in New Jersey," Monsieur Dauphin said. "No one is surprised that I am married to an American girl who is so much younger than I am, but everyone is surprised I live in New Jersey."

Monsieur Dauphin, who has been married twice before—both times to French girls—said: "You have a feeling of great security when you marry an American girl. The alimony is so high in the United States that you know you can't afford to get a divorce."

Monsieur Dauphin lives in the town of Elberon, outside of Asbury Park.

"It's a very nice community, and I've become very involved in local activities. The only thing is that I can't become a member of the volunteer fire department—first, because I'm not a citizen, and second, because they don't think an actor is serious enough to put out a fire."

With his vast experience in marriage on both sides of the ocean, Monsieur Dauphin can talk with authority about the difference between the two tribes.

He said it wasn't hard to adjust to an American wife after being married to two French ones.

"The American woman is more independent and perhaps more demanding, but I have always been in love with women, so I think they should have everything."

It is only when it comes to their attitude toward sin that the two nationalities differ, he said.

"The French consider living in sin charming. There is nothing wrong with having a mistress, and it has not only been accepted in France for a long time but celebrated in all of French literature.

"Once I was asked on the Mike Wallace show how the French, a nation of Catholics, could reconcile their attitude toward extramarital affairs with their religion. I didn't know the answer at the time, but I've been thinking about it ever since, and now I believe I know.

"The Frenchman thinks he is the only one in the world who has a special agreement with God—that God will forgive him because he likes the French so much. The Frenchman feels he is so amusing and intelligent that God must surely allow him a few licenses.

"If he eats meat on Friday he says: 'God knows I have a bad liver, and, after all, He doesn't want all this good food and wine to go to waste.'

"In America, there is a religion about morality. To live in sin publicly is quite wrong. Even in Hollywood it's objectionable to have official liaisons with women without marriage. Errol Flynn had a special dispensation, but all the others had to marry—and divorce, of course—to satisfy Louella Parsons.

"American TV glorifies married couples. I don't think *I Love Lucy* would have been such a success if Lucy and Desi hadn't been married. Now they've broken up, and the country is in mourning. In France, if a couple that has been together for a long, long time breaks up, there is general rejoicing. The French get fed up with something romantic that lasts too long."

Monsieur Dauphin said that there was one advantage to being married to a Frenchwoman over an American woman, and that was that Frenchwomen—so far—do not have access to charge accounts.

"You can control your wife better in France," he continued. "In the United States, the American wife is constantly being tempted to spend more than her husband earns. The whole psychology of the supermarket is to let her buy things without anybody watching her.

"Every time three housewives are seen doing nothing in a neighborhood, they build a department store next to them.

"In the United States, everyone is trying to make the American woman sin economically. They don't mind if a woman has an affair with her supermarket or department store, and everybody is working to make the American woman taste the forbidden apple.

"In France, a woman can sin if she wants to—as long as she's pure in her dealings with the money she spends for the family."

The Best Stories of the Year

EVERY year the wire services list the best stories of the year, Unfortunately there are many on the back pages of newspapers that never make the headlines.

Here is my own list of the best stories of the year.

Wayne Cartwright drove a taxi for twenty-five years and never made more than seventy-five dollars a week. He always dreamed of some day making a fortune, but Wayne knew that as a cab driver he would probably die poor. One day he was cleaning out his cab, when he found behind his seat a diamond necklace. Wayne thought it looked like a piece of costume jewelry, and he gave it to his ten-year-old daughter to play with. A few weeks later a friend was visiting the house and noticed the necklace. The friend said to Wayne: "I think the necklace is real."

Wayne and his wife became very excited and the next day they rushed down to the jewelry store with the necklace. The jeweler studied it for several minutes and then looked up at the couple, smiled, and said: "The necklace is just a piece of costume jewelry and not worth anything." Wayne gave the necklace back to his daughter, who plays with it every day.

A Yorkshire chimney sweep named Roger Hogsworth used to play the English football pools every week for sixpence. One day he was at home picking the teams that would win when his two-year-old son, who was playing with a pin, marked up a form and accidentally made a series of selections. When Roger saw the form, he tore up his own selections and sent in the ones made by his son, who had no idea what he was doing.

When the results were printed in the newspaper the next day Roger discovered that every selection his son had made was wrong, but every one he himself had made before he tore up his own form was correct. If Roger Hogsworth had sent in his own selections instead of his son's he would have won £150,000.

Little Gerard Kelly, aged ten, was having difficulty in history and was about to fail the subject. His last assignment was to write a paper on World War II.

Gerard decided the man who knew more about World War II than anybody else was Sir Winston Churchill, and so, unbeknownst to his teacher and his parents, he wrote to the former Prime Minister explaining his problem and asking Sir Winston if he would write to him and tell him what he thought was the turning point of World War II.

Much to Gerard's surprise, Sir Winston never answered his letter, and Gerard had to take the course over again.

Chuck Winthrop, who weighed only 140 pounds, was too light to make the Wallaboo University football team, but he tried so hard that the coach took pity on him and let him suit up every game, though he always kept him on the bench.

In the final game of the year against Wallaboo's archrivals, Gazonga Tech, Wallaboo's first-string quarterback was injured in the second quarter. In the final quarter Wallaboo's second-string quarterback was also injured. Gazonga was leading 6-0.

The coach looked down the bench and his eyes met Chuck's.

"Please, coach," pleaded Chuck. "My parents came two thousand miles to see me play. Send me in."

The coach shook his head. "You're too light."

"It's my last year. Just let me play for a few minutes," Chuck cried.

The coach got up from the bench and walked over to Chuck. He put his hand on his shoulder and he said: "No, you're too light. We'll finish up the game without a quarter-back."

And Wallaboo did. The final score was still 6-0.

John F. Kelly was young, personable, rich, and a top-flight politician. He had served in the House of Representatives and then went on to win a tough Senate race.

Last spring he went to his father and said: "I'd like to run for the Presidency of the United States."

His father said: "Son, a Catholic could never win the Presidency. Come into the business with me."

So Kelly resigned from the Senate and went into business with his father.

THIS BOOK WAS SET IN

CALEDONIA, NICOLAS COCHIN,

AND COCHIN ITALIC TYPES BY

V AND M TYPOGRAPHERS.

IT WAS PRINTED AT THE PRESS OF

THE WORLD PUBLISHING COMPANY.

DESIGN IS BY LARRY KAMP